M000300199

TIME PASSING

. . . . .

European Perspectives

EUROPEAN PERSPECTIVES

A Series in Social Thought and Cultural Criticism
Lawrence D. Kritzman, Editor

European Perspectives presents outstanding books
by leading European thinkers. With both classic
and contemporary works, the series aims to shape
the major intellectual controversies of our day and to
facilitate the tasks of historical understanding.

*For a complete list of books in the series,
see pages 213–16.*

TIME PASSING · MODERNITY AND NOSTALGIA

SYLVIANE AGACINSKI

translated by Jody Gladding

Columbia University Press   New York

Columbia University Press wishes to express its
appreciation for assistance given by the government
of France through the Ministère de la Culture
in the preparation of this translation.

COLUMBIA UNIVERSITY PRESS
PUBLISHERS SINCE 1893
New York   Chichester, West Sussex

French edition © 2000 Editions du Seuil
Collection La Librairie du XXe siècle, sous la direction de
Maurice Olender
Translation copyright © 2003 Columbia University Press
All rights reserved

Library of Congress Cataloging-in-Publication Data
Agacinski, Sylviane.
[Passeur de temps. English]
Time passing : modernity and nostalgia / Sylviane Agacinski ;
translated by Jody Gladding.
p.   cm. — (European perspectives)
Includes bibliographical references and index.
ISBN 0-231-12514-3 (cloth : alk. paper) — ISBN 0-231-12515-1 (pbk.)
1. Time. I. Title. II. Series.
BD638 .A27713 2003
304.2'3—dc21
2002031451

Columbia University Press books are printed on permanent
and durable acid-free paper.
Printed in the United States of America

c 10 9 8 7 6 5 4 3 2 1
p 10 9 8 7 6 5 4 3 2 1

Contents

. . . . .

Illustrations

. . . . .

1. Anonymous, *Group of students with their model*, ca. 1890–
   1900. Aristotype, 24.6 × 34.2 cm. École nationale supérieure
   des beaux-arts, Paris.
2. Oscar Gustav Rejlander, *The head of Saint John the Baptist*,
   1856. Print on albuminated paper using two negatives, 10.7
   × 15.1 cm. Royal Photographic Society, Bath.
3. William Lake Price, *Robinson Crusoe and Friday*, 1855–56.
   Print on albuminated paper, 25 × 30 cm. Private collection.
4. Julia Margaret Cameron, *King Ahasuerus and Queen Esther*,
   1865. Print on albuminated paper, 31.7 × 27.1 cm. National
   Museum of Photography, Film and Television, Bradford.
5. Julia Margaret Cameron, *Saint Agnes*, 1864. Print on albuminated paper, 27 × 20 cm. National Museum of Photography,
   Film and Television, Bradford.
6. Henry Peach Robinson, *Fading Away*, 1858. Print on albuminated paper using five negatives, 23.8 × 37.9 cm. Royal Photographic Society, Bath.

Translator's Note

. . . . .

THROUGHOUT the French text, the author plays with the many meanings of the French word *épreuve*. The word itself occurs frequently, sometimes two or three times in a paragraph or on a page. The literal meaning of *épreuve* is "test," "ordeal," "trial," "hardship." It can also mean "experience" (from the verb *éprouver*, to experience) or "proof." It is used to refer to both page proofs in printing and photographic proofs. The French title for the first section of this book is "*Épreuves du temps*," which I have translated as "Tests of Time," obviously less resonant than the original. When readers come across any of these various translations of *épreuve*, they should bear in mind that the author's rich semantic play has been sacrificed for the sake of fluent English. For the same reason and at the author's request, I have retained masculine pronouns throughout.

TIME PASSING
. . . . .

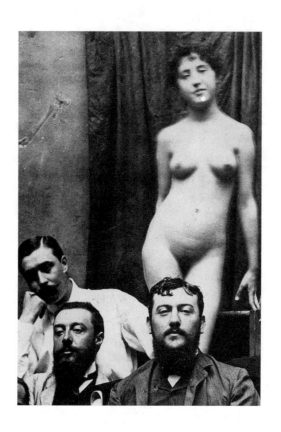

THE "MODEL" moved slightly, blurring the features of her face. So who is this naked young woman, exposing herself triumphantly above a group of serious, bearded students?*

This is no longer Venus emerging from the wave but a singular young woman—Marie or Juliette, we can't say. For a moment, she has stopped posing for the painters, who have turned modestly away from her charming unclothed body, strange among all those suits and ties. While the artists in the studio pose with a learned air (they think they are the main subjects of the photo), she looks confidently into the camera. She guesses that soon we are going to see her for what she is, here and now. At that moment, she knows that she is no longer a *model* but the subject of a new image.

This young woman, whose photographic image still reaches us in all its freshness, we will call *modernity*.

THE WESTERN HOUR

· · · · ·

Is IT EVER possible to think about one's own time? The present
emerges amid the shadows of a past that no longer evokes nostalgia and an uncertain future. A glance at neither the past nor the
future can reveal the meaning of the present. We endlessly repeat
the question of time as if it only just appeared in all its force since
the retreat of what softened its tragic aspect: eternity and a sense
of history. Against the background of this retreat, history reveals
its contingency and our naked relationship to passage. Can the
idea of epoch still hold meaning for us?

An Invisible Present

In Western history, epochs have been conceived as very large
"slices" of time corresponding to *worlds*, each presenting a certain
unity, like antiquity or the Middle Ages. Hegel still divides world
history into *worlds*—Oriental, Greek, Roman, Germanic—that are
so many stages (*Stufengang*) in the history of Reason. These worlds

not only succeed one another and advance through time, but they also are organized geographically from east to west.[1]

The events (like the French Revolution) meant to usher in new times are themselves conditioned by an invisible maturation and the slow death throes of the preceding period. Thus the ancient world gradually collapsed before the Christian world was established. According to Hegel's lovely formulation "The continuous crumbling that has not altered the look of things at all is suddenly interrupted by the rising of the sun, which, in a flash, designs with one stroke the shape of the new world."[2]

Without reviewing the Hegelian understanding of the idea of universal history—the most powerful yet to be conceived—let us remember that the teleological rationality that reconciles reason with time is fully realized there.

Hegel warned his audience: philosophical thought "has no goal other than to eliminate chance."[3] There is no true place, then, for *contingency* in human affairs. The final end of the world gives meaning to this history of which men themselves are not yet conscious but toward which they advance. Beginning with the Christian conception of history, the "epochs" appeared as stages within an overall progression, as steps that humanity had to mount in order to rise toward the good and its true end. But the teleological principle according to which the world's progress would achieve one final goal (its *telos*), whether presented from a religious or a metaphysical perspective, has worn thin, giving way to, taken as a whole, a more or less random and disoriented history.

I will not consider again here the different ways of thinking about the epochs or periods of Western history. This question has already been covered remarkably well by Krzysztof Pomian.[4] In this book, I will examine only certain aspects of modern thinking about time and its genesis, in particular the relationship of time to movement. I will then turn my attention to the experience of images, so distinctive today, to see in what ways they constitute a new test of time. Finally, I will consider the conflicts of *tempos* that arise today between political temporality and the compression of time to which the logic of the media leads.

The idea of epoch is linked to that of world, just as time is inseparable from space. The hypothesis of a time that is ours—that is, the time of this world—presents itself as soon as we say *we*, as soon as we evoke a community of a "generation" with that plural subject. We want very much to see this world's face and to define its contours. But only images, not the ambient world in which we live, have *borders*. The reality of the present is as impossible to *frame* as are the contours of a place through ordinary means of perception. It is the historian's job to hold up the mirror afterward to reflect the face of an epoch that its contemporaries could not perceive.

Religions, states, and empires have nevertheless defined the principal historical frameworks that allow us to demarcate extended epochs, worlds, and civilizations. Traditionally, religion and politics have constituted the two orders in relation to which time could be divided and calculated. They had their defining events, such as the coming of a prophet or a god, the birth of a dynasty, the conquest of an empire. History was religious and political, and "time" was, too. But history has ceased to be organized by these two great forces.

Since the nineteenth century, the world's technical development has constituted the primary referential field for describing and organizing the whole of human societies. Henceforth, technical advances alone will determine the hierarchy of societies, which, by means of the global establishment of that same imperative for development, are integrated into a world and a unique time. Globalization is the unification of the world's rhythms, all adjusted to the Western clock, that is, to contemporary chronotechnology.

In all domains, it is the technical order that provides the fundamental standards for classifying societies, as if in the final analysis,

Western rationality had dominated all other worlds of thought—as in the Middle Ages when the time of the markets gained precedence over the time of the church.[5]

 Through the techniques by which time is measured and through its assimilation as a market value, we can witness the Western hour's hold over the entire world. Enfolded in our time, distinct and distant societies are now inscribed into our own history. The technical hegemony of the West expresses itself all over the world through the extension of production methods and the establishment of its temporal architecture. But it is not only the measure of time that has been unified; it is also its value, reduced to the market value of work time. Western rationality has deployed an economics according to which time must be productive, useful, and profitable. We must forever "gain time," because time itself gains us something else. That is why *to give* our time, to spend it or lose it, to let it pass, are now the only ways of resisting the general economy of time.

This economy is no longer only characteristic of Western societies; it has taken over the planet. Even though we move about more and more, it is nearly as difficult to travel in space (that is, to change surroundings, to be displaced) as it is to change time or rhythm. For Lévi-Strauss, anthropology could still fall back on a "displacement" technique and demand that we not apply our categories to so-called primitive societies (that is, societies without writing). Our gaze on societies *distant in space* was not supposed to reduce those societies to being *distant in time*, as in the old eth-nocentric and historicist manner, which interpreted any gap as a delay. Differentialist anthropology thus renounced an evolutionist vision, marked by colonialist ambitions, that saw remote societies as *backward* societies, destined to catch up with *us*.

Nevertheless, even if the criticism of ethnocentrism has lost none of its theoretical relevance, we refer less and less to the close and the distant in space or to any lags in time. As a planetwide technological empire, globalization has brought together the regions of the world and made its societies into contemporaries.[6]

"Primitive" societies have disappeared or are confined to museumlike reserves where they gradually lose their culture. The imperative for development, imposed on all continents, is absolute, so that it takes the form of an almost unquestioned shared ethic. And because it is both *universal* and *unequal*, technological development has become the measure of all societies. Military and industrial power is adopted as the goal everywhere, and it is no longer possible for a Westerner to be *displaced*. Everywhere he finds himself at home, with the same religion of technological development, the same logic of profit, the same economics of time, and even the same "local crafts," factory made and sold to tourists in all countries. Ethnocentrism has disappeared because it has been realized.

All countries are subject to the same logic, whether they are called *developing* (to avoid a "politically incorrect" expression), *underdeveloped*, or *emerging* (if they are a bit more "advanced"). But just as medications often bring with them "undesirable" side effects, enthusiasm for the logic of power, associated with the craze for profit, leads to all sorts of perverse effects: the destruction of ecological, economic, or social stability. Pollution, unemployment, migration, and the breakdown of societies are some of the consequences of "technological progress," which must henceforth be distinguished from mere "progress" by itself.

Slow Down History?

It has become difficult for us, therefore, to believe in a rational evolution of the world. Progress seems neither universal nor certain to us. This suspicion could change our conception of time and ward off our impatience: to what are we endlessly hurrying, so eager for change? And at the height of the movement that pushes us forward, what if the need to *temporize* were to become apparent? Quietly—it is true—imperceptibly, we await the future less, and it can be tempting to slow down history.

Lévi-Strauss's intelligent analyses can help guide us here to the extent that they have shown how the value given to change varies according to society. Just as our Western societies seem *made for change*—because they believe in the possibility of indefinitely increasing their knowledge and their power—likewise so-called primitive societies have only one goal, *enduring* and maintaining an equilibrium between humans and between humans and nature.

This division between "hot" and "cold" societies could make us consider the difference, always cropping up in our societies, between the "progressives" and the "conservatives"—which does not mean, as Marc Augé rightly pointed out, between the left and the right.[7]

This is because the conservatives are not always and not only on the right, and those devoted to progress or modernization can defend interests that are not at all "leftist." From a social or cultural perspective, this or that advance is sometimes paid for by losses more serious than the gains. Thus, resisting the social effects of economic liberalism can make the left appear "conservative" in a new sense.

No political thinking in our cultures is, however, "conservative" in the sense that traditional societies could be. We cannot imagine ourselves removed from history, that is, from events that, even without progress, irreversibly transform the world and create the possibility for something new. For us, time remains *one way*, even if we do not know where that way is leading. Conversely, societies that "refuse to accept history," in Lévi-Strauss's words, are those that live with reference to a mythic order that is itself *outside time*. Resistant to novelty, primitive "conservatism" is driven by a concern for maintaining balances, especially the balance between the human and the natural worlds—an idea long foreign to modern Western thinking, except among the ancient Greeks.

If reference to an extratemporal order has become foreign to us, the need for maintaining balances or harmony is once again becoming clear through that modern concern for *conservation* that has nothing to do with the old political conservatism, but with worries over what must be *preserved*, what deserves to endure, as much as what must change. The valorization of protection expresses itself through the valorization of our cultural or natural heritage, the environment, or in the "precautionary principle." It has become legitimate to wonder about history and how it has accelerated, to want to check certain movements if the drawbacks of the new are often more serious than its advantages. When progress reveals itself to be the "wheel with double gears" that "makes something go by crushing something else," according to Victor Hugo, we cannot look away from those it neglects or the values it destroys.

After having conquered the planet and imposed its technoeconomic imperative throughout, the West now harbors a need to resist the unconditional ideal of change, or "progress," that breaks with the forward flight of yesterday's modernism and avant-garde ideas.

Nevertheless, this new relationship to time, reinforced by the memory of this century's disasters, is not tied up with any nostalgia and does not idealize the past. In this book, you will not find a complaint against the technoscientific era or a hymn to the pastoral world of days gone by. Much invention is needed to safeguard what deserves to last, and technology can still correct its

own faults—on the condition that it not be subjected to the logic of profit alone. It is not the watches that impose the profitable use of time on the world; it is the impatience of the stock markets awaiting their profits.

We have no means of escaping temporality or history. But tested by an ephemeral world subject to dazzling metamorphoses, we recognize that time is an assistant to both good and evil. We can neither predict the future nor have faith in it, since in any case, things do not happen as we want. Thus it is necessary to "navigate by sight," to agree to experiment with the short term and in limited areas. The certitude that no one can calculate tomorrow's global effects of decisions made today—even if attempts at such calculations are vital—is one of the reasons that we urge a slowdown of history. But is this possible, and how? To the general economy of time, we would like to oppose the value of time itself, that is, of the time we agree to spend, to let pass, to lose.

Each generation is called on anew to experience the test of time. But what does *to pass* mean for us if neither eternity nor history any longer gives meaning to that passage? The vertiginous effect of the worlds' irreversibility is mitigated only by the possibility of enduring, which is the fruit of repetition and reproduction.

In the contemporary world, technology is expanding the possibilities of repetition in an unprecedented fashion, and nature offers the models for it. Beyond the economic consequences of industrial means for reproducing certain merchandise in great quantities, the possibility of producing and multiplying images offers one of the strangest forms of repetition. Our world, overpopulated by images, makes us live among crowds of phantoms and doubt the homogeneity of our times.

PASSAGE

. . . . .

MODERN CONSCIOUSNESS is one of *passage* and the *passing*.
From now on we think that everything *arrives* and *passes*. Nothing permanent gives things any kind of anchor against time. The
movements that sweep the world along cannot even be unified, being too numerous and distinct and following different rhythms.
Does this increase in flux still leave us a time that is truly ours?
Can *passage* make an epoch, or does it compromise even any possibility of present? It is all the more necessary to speak of *modern
times* in the plural, since permanent facts seem lacking, those stable forms that would trace the outline of an unchanging land-
scape, capable of giving modernity a face. Thus, it must have
many of them, and if it designates an experience of *passage* and of
the *passing*, of movement and of the ephemeral, of fluctuation and
of the mortal, modernity does not renounce eternity alone, it also
renounces a unique form of temporality and of history.

The *passing* is no longer a moment in a continuous history di-
rected toward an end—a single step on a ladder that needs only to

be climbed to attain the final summit—but a *one-way passage* to which one blindly commits oneself. In search of the present time, we meet the gaze of Walter Benjamin as Theodor W. Adorno describes it: "His philosophical interest never focuses on what has no history, but always on what is the most determined by time, on the irreversible. From which derives the title, *One Way Street*."[1] Thus history advances without a final destination.

The idea of a history aimed toward its end, such as prevailed since the eighteenth century, gave meaning to the ephemeral as a necessary stage in universal progress, whereas our time can neither orient itself beginning with the past nor wait for the future to give it meaning. Modernity—ours today—no longer belongs to a "regime of historicity" for which history is written "from the point of view of the future."[2] We will see here that modern temporality is the endless interlacing of the irreversible and the repetitive.

But modernity has also broken with the eternal. As an alternative to the exclusive valorization of what lasts, what remains, or what could one day come to completion, we may have no other choice anymore but to accept the passing, even to commend the futile. Having become strangers to the ancient dreams, it remains for us to consider "passingness," to accept the *lightness* of what *passes*. At the beginning of the twentieth century, Freud invited us to embrace the *Vergänglichkeit*—the "passingness" of things that, according to the classical vision, could not have meaning in themselves and necessarily referred back to an eternal order. Freudian praise for *Vergänglichkeit* is a response to the Angels of the *Second Faust*, whom Goethe makes say, "*Alles Vergängliche ist nur ein Gleichnis*—All the ephemeral is only allegory,"[3] as if this world's transient beings can never find their meaning *here*, in themselves, but only in a beyond, in the realm of God; as if what happens in the temporal and transient order of the perceptible world can acquire meaning or truth only from a being who absolutely transcends time and the world's changes.

Indeed, according to a long tradition—from which it is difficult to break—the *passing* has been conceived as the negation of the eternal and thus of being. From its beginning, philosophy has identified being with permanence, timelessness, whereas the passing, the ephemeral, is cast out into nonbeing and stripped of all value. Thus, the relationship of the eternal to the temporal is analogous to that of being and appearance, the intelligible and the sensible. According to this structure, Platonic in origin, being itself can never *pass*, in any sense of the word; it cannot move from one place to another, as a bird *passes* through the sky, or end or die, or both appear and disappear.

But to say of the eternal that it does not *pass* is to say that it does not *arrive* either; its transcendence is also that very absence of sensible manifestation, that impossibility of actually *arriving* in the world. This, in effect, explains the permanently *allegorical* relationship of the temporal to the eternal and, more generally, the absence of being, meaning, and, finally, value for everything that passes. For all that, the greatest beauty is called on to die, even though it has value and existence.

"The Foretaste of Mourning"

We can experience the passing nature of being, things, institutions, and nature itself. This experience is well known, very old, well established. Perhaps it is inevitably painful, but as Freud says, "What is painful can also be true."[4] Thus it is necessary to accept the pain of loss when it arises, instead of a priori scorning the pleasure of the ephemeral and succumbing to the "foretaste of mourning." There is nothing that can promise to eradicate the trial of loss, or its pain, except the assertion that it would be absurd to anticipate the time of mourning, to suffer it in advance, and to deprive oneself of the pleasure of the present. Better to say goodbye to what no longer is, to resist the melancholy distaste that the ruin of things can inspire, and to ignore the—illusory—consolation found in the denial of death. Whether one abandons oneself to melancholy sadness and the foretaste of mourning or seeks refuge in the vain hope of eternity, in each case one turns from the real: what is there, in the process of (coming to pass and) passing.[5] The anticipation of death, which we cannot help thinking about, has two possible effects: melancholy, which withdraws any present from us in advance and, conversely, love for finite things or beings, all the more intense since it is hopeless.

Though in some ways it is incompatible, the thinking of both Kierkegaard and Nietzsche confronts finitude: the first, to maintain the singular trial that it implies and to resist the mollifying temptations of speculation but without abandoning nostalgia for the eternal, and, the second, to avoid all suffering by the cruel affirmation of the tragic and praise for oblivion.

Nietzsche and Freud remain out of step with time insofar as they taught the value of oblivion, whereas memory's demands and incessant commemorations weigh more than ever on our shoulders. We would be nothing without the past generations, nothing without their history and our own, but memory is accurate only if it gives meaning to present existence. Life has always needed forgetfulness more than memory, and even the desire for commemorative monuments satisfies the desire to entrust memory to material reminders—to better free us from the past. Forgetting their parents' past is each new generation's right.

No one has any chance of denying the universal transience of things, but it is futile to rebel against it or to find in it a reason for disgust. Passing can also be beautiful, on the condition of upholding, without regret, the *retreat of the eternal*. We understand this retreat as a modern disappearance but also as a permanent feature: the eternal is always and necessarily *in retreat* from the mortals that we are. It has always been so, and that is why identifying being with the eternal was a necessary part of nostalgia.

The retreat of the eternal is not new; it is modern only because of its rupture with nostalgia.

The "passingness" of things is also experienced today through modern forms of representation. It was for representing perishable things that images were first condemned, branded with the seal of illusion. In this sense, the question of the image always involves the question of being: if being stops being eternal and if passing acquires ontological dignity, then the images of a transitory world can themselves emerge from the shadow of nonbeing and become capable of truth.

According to the way we see it, the world seems made up of incessant movements of which we perceive only certain periods, or *sequences*. The image in movement—from film to video and digital—has become the technological model for our experience: images pass, like things and events, according to a continuous movement from which we sometimes extract some artificially arrested scene. Truth refers to movement. The fixed is the exception, the mobile is the rule. Far from taking any sort of precedence over the *mobile*, the *immobile* is a simple *pause*, a suspension of time.

This permanent kinetic flux is animated by an infinite number of movements, that is, by different temporalities and also by separate rhythms. Not only does nothing escape time, but there also are an infinite number of times, or *tempos*, which makes it hard for us to define an epoch, or a history, since they go together.

To define an epoch, the forms of a world must present a certain homogeneity and sufficient stability. Also, beyond its own specific nature, the epoch must be inscribed in a historic whole of which it constitutes a part. It assumes a continuity of time, or history, on whose horizon it outlines its own figure. It constitutes a singular moment within a large temporal unity. As we have noted, the idea of epoch thus forms one system with the idea of universal history. As *total* movement—past, present, and to come—history unified what the temporality of the world seemed to dismantle. From a corrupting factor, time for humanity became the condition for its fulfillment. As the time of a single movement, it satisfied the desire to reconcile the immutable eternal with the rupture of temporal movements, the timeless infinite with the finite nature of passing things, the one with the many.

But in its turn, historical time, which at first replaced the eternal or cyclical order, became fragmented. The eternal allowed being to be thought of as *permanent*, beyond the apparent transformations of beings, whereas occurrence made it seem *unstable*, in the chemical sense of the term. History's trick—the philosophical concept of history—was to imagine that a single substance could be both lost and found again in time.

When philosophy stops opposing the eternal and the temporal and considers, with Hegel, the engagement of being in time, it attempts to save temporal beings from the *disappearance* to which they are doomed. History, as overarching movement and as full account, tries to restore the unity of being, shattered by time.

By radically taking on finitude, modern thought has abandoned the continuity of history. Of course, if being is what happens "in time," we cannot do without the idea of history, but events have ceased to be inscribed in a comprehensive movement and no longer seem organized according to a unique direction or a single meaning.

Like change, time always *makes* and *unmakes*[6] "at the same time." Advances and declines are contemporaneous with each other; births and deaths are both daughters of time. History becomes disoriented.

Nostalgia

Ever since Plato and the metaphysical condemnation of the ephemeral, philosophy has been stricken with nostalgia—that is, a painful feeling of exile, the homesickness that the Germans call

Heimweh, the feeling that wherever one is, one is not *at home.*
The forms of this nostalgia change, but it remains the expression
of a kind of religious or metaphysical thinking that is fundamentally dualist. Thus, according to Plato, the body and the world to
which it belongs constitute that place where the soul is far from
its origin. The soul is not "at home" in the body that makes it
prisoner; it is its tomb, just as the world is its cave, and it aspires
to find its true place again, the place of ideas, the world of the intelligible. Philosophy must free the soul from the body to which
it is bound. Every pleasure and every pain, Socrates told Phaedo,
"nails the soul to the body," which can deliver itself from this jail
only through death.[7]

For his part, Heidegger defined the "fundamental tonality" of
philosophy as nostalgia: "We who philosophize are away from
home everywhere," he wrote.[8] However, modern man no longer
feels even this nostalgia natural to the finite being, because he has
lost the sense of what true habitation means: "The contemporary
city dweller, ape of civilization, hasn't he for a long time now been
rid of nostalgia?"[9] Paradoxically, this modern city dweller, the
simple imitator of civilized men of the past, the barbaric "ape"
who no longer knows how to dwell, does not know what he has
lost and does not suffer from it. He has rid himself of all nostalgia, and the word itself has lost its meaning in everyday life. It is
not the feeling of being at home that defines an authentic way of
inhabiting, that lyrical manner of dwelling by welcoming with
hospitality the earth or the being—without seeking to take technological possession of it—rather, it is homesickness, nostalgia,
that can show whether modern man, aware of his exile, still
knows what "inhabiting" means.

There are many ways of thinking about or experiencing exile.
Heidegger's way dives into the romantic idealization of ancient
rural culture and into making the earth and rootedness sacred,
which evokes the thinking and the *pathos* of Spengler in *The De-*

cline of the West. The motifs of the fall, of the unfortunate "depropriation," of nostalgia, even of exile, are the mark of religious or metaphysical thinking that condemns the present world. Modernity is thus synonymous with decline as we find in Spengler, with time appearing as a factor in regression and oblivion, whereas searching for originary authenticity has become the fundamental orientation for thinking, as is the case in Heidegger.

Thus, while Cartesian or Hegelian modernity is characterized by establishing thought within its *own* world, excluding all nostalgia, modern man, according to Heidegger, experiences an exile and an uprooting so profound that he is not even aware of it and loses all feelings of nostalgia. It certainly is difficult today not to suffer permanent displacement (historical even more than geographical), but all displacement, however unnerving, is not necessarily *nostalgic.* One is not required to search origins like a lost homeland. People today can no longer feel peacefully established in a world that is their own, as Cartesian or Hegelian philosophies still permitted them to do, but they are no longer pious enough to suffer from exile.

An Ethic of the Ephemeral

Forever beginning again, modernity makes reference to the present, not as a simple portion of time, but as what time alone can *give*: the *passing* or, again, as Baudelaire writes, the "contingent" and the "circumstantial."[10] In breaking with the classical, timeless ideal, the modernity of art (the poet's only interest) thus implies a valorization of the passing, from fashion to the larger sense of the word. Baudelaire defines the modern artist as one who knows how to see and to perpetuate the beauty of his own time. Therefore, if they bear the particular mark of their epoch, the works of the past can also be called modern. Modernity never stops referring to the present of the one who attempts to define it, on the condition that he knows how to take into account this present, to seize the truth and the necessity of the moment. This taking into account implies no progressive vision of the future but only a sense of the uniqueness of a situation, even of an opportune moment, what the Greeks called *kairòs.* Thus it is not necessary to relegate the terms *modern* and *modernity* to this or that period of history, since each one has its moderns.

It is not sufficient, therefore, for a work to be current for it to be of its time. The academic replication of old works cannot be called modern. The value of modernity, if there is one, is awarded to works that cannot belong to other times.

This is not the value of the universal: it presupposes the fecundity of time, in other words, the possibility that occurrence innovates and surprises instead of submitting to the universality of a law. Law programs the necessity of events—whether it is given as a law of identical repetition or as a law of a teleological process, that is, of an order establishing itself progressively.

We cannot think about modernity without recognizing the random part of occurrence, the singular nature of situations and the breakdown of law. Thus, if Kantian philosophy remains deeply estranged from the idea of modernity as we understand it, it is because it claims to forever extricate the *unconditional* and methodically to exclude the empirical *conditions* for a decision or an action. Kantian thinking fundamentally tends to avoid occurrence, even to resist it, obstinately, as the strangest ethics a philosopher could ever conceive proves: one entailing a duty based on the universality of the law, to the point of remaining indifferent to the actual consequences of an act.

An ethics and a politics of the ephemeral, on the contrary, would require thinking about the actual effects of a choice and, in relations with others, taking account of situations and peculiarities. They would not be the thinking of the moment but of the present, that is, of the relationship between movements and durations.

The relative contingency of occurrence does not rule out, however, either repetitions or recurrences; rather, these are combined with the new. The irregular springs from the heart of the regular, or conversely, the old returns to the heart of the new. The new is lodged in the old, the original in the reproduction. In this sense, no world is homogeneous, and this heterogeneity produces anachronisms.

The idea of modernity refers less to a situation in time than it is itself *a certain way of thinking about time,* free from both eternity and so-called historical *necessity.* It leads to the demand for thinking in time, with occurrence, and not in spite of it, in a vain quest for the absolute.

With the assumption of his finitude and his contingency, resigning himself to the "short view," modern man puts truth back in the present, even if this present, far from being presented in the light, emerges from the shadow that envelopes the past and the future. Modern consciousness is no longer that of the Enlightenment but, rather, the recognition of having to think and decide within the limits of a certain present, with its share of obscurity.

No One Can See Oneself Dead

Montaigne invented modernity in literature by giving up relating truth to the timeless: "I do not paint being. I paint passage: not the passage from age to age or, as people say, from seven years to seven years, but from day to day, from minute to minute. One must accommodate the history of the hour."[11]

Descartes invented modern philosophy by leaving behind the old nostalgia and asserting the autonomy of thinking that uses itself as a starting point. "Here we are at home," Hegel said of him, meaning that with Descartes, we enter into modern thought, which consists precisely of beginning with itself and finally feeling *at home.* This *at home* no longer means the same thing today; it rules out returning to a metaphysical or religious position turned toward an absolute *beyond*. As opposed to all neo-Kantism, modern philosophers confront the empirical conditions for truth in many different ways. Maurice Merleau-Ponty expressed this rupture of philosophy with transcendence and law by asserting, "The philosophical absolute holds no seat anywhere, thus it is never elsewhere, it must be defended on each occasion."[12]

The nostalgic tone is absent in Hegel, as in Descartes, because philosophy puts absolute transcendence on "home leave." By believing himself capable of surmounting the ruptures of finitude, however, Hegel is a philosopher of time, one who expresses the temporality of thought and being and one who believes thought capable of overcoming time.

Indeed, it was with *The Phenomenology of Spirit* that ephemeral reality was awarded its highest ontological value. Since the absolute presents itself by entering into temporality and since time is the destiny and the necessity of the spirit, one can say of the absolute that it *passes*—a scandalous formula, metaphysically speaking. Being itself is no longer beyond time, or outside all time, that is, eternal; it exists in its own *passage*.

For the speculative dialectic, though, there cannot be *pure* passage. Even if the future does not come to an end in a definitive and timeless presence, it gathers itself together dialectically in the unity of a "subject" (of history) that claims temporalization and differentiation as *its own*. *Passing* acquires its reality as the moment of becoming only with the subjective execution of a synthesis of time. By what means is this synthesis executed? Differentiation and temporalization are yielded to the unity of being that temporalizes *itself* and self-differentiates (itself). The eye of the philosopher seems to witness the passage of being, just as the Christian God, that authoritative mirror, "appeared temporally before himself."[13] This gaze must transcend or overcome its own passage to gather from it the truth, at each moment, in each epoch, and also, finally, once and for all, all at the same time. To salvage what passes, the eye of the spirit, or the philosopher's gaze, must itself become an absolute eye, capable of *seeing its own passage*, simultaneously engaged in time and assembling time, simultaneously passing and not passing.

This philosophical feat, enough to make the baron of Münchhausen pull out his hair, clearly represents the idea of a mind capable of being in time and surmounting its temporality. But if one can describe the individual consciousness as truly capable of simultaneously existing in time and recalling its own past, how can the spirit raise itself above its present and its epoch to a position from which it can take in the entire memory of the world? Finite human thought extends widely beyond its own time, no doubt, thanks to what it is capable of inheriting from earlier generations. But the traces and the remains that generations inherit with their bodies and their culture constitute enigmas more than conscious experience, more opaque than penetrable.

The *modern pathos* is no longer the triumph of autonomous thought but the recognition that thought is rooted in the non-thought that constitutes our inheritance and that we can no longer absolutely appropriate (for example, biological, economic, and linguistic inheritance). Thus as Foucault writes, man "lodges his thinking within the folds of a language so much older than he is that he cannot master the meanings of it brought back to life, nevertheless, by the insistence of his speech."[14] Modern consciousness cannot skirt these "a priori histories" to appropriate their origins and foundations. We cannot flatten out these *folds*, whose hollows we live in.

These questions already animate the spirit of Kierkegaardian, Nietzschian, and Freudian resistance to the dialectical ambition, each calling into question human thought's claim of overcoming its finitude, that is, its birth, history, and death.

The dialectic speaks to us again, however, if while rereading Hegel as passing's thinker, the philosophical eye—far from being

interpreted as "an overarching figure"—becomes the requirement
for an always present philosophical regard, in every epoch, at
each moment, requiring for itself a grasp on its passing. Jean-Luc
Nancy thus pointed out what could be a kind of modern
Hegelianism.[15] But then the *absolute* subject overcoming its own
deaths must be renounced and thus an essential part of the speculative dialectic.

The thinking regarding time, that is, the thinking that knows
how to grapple with its own temporality and finitude, is thinking
that accepts "seeing" neither the past nor the future. It is thinking
that thinks about—but as the places of its own mystery—its birth
and its death, because no one can see oneself being born or dying.

We cannot see the world through the eyes of our ancestors—
anymore than they can see it through ours. It is an illusion of universalism and the philosophy of history that believes it is possible
to erase the *generational difference*. Because what is time if not
that necessity according to which the generations give birth to one
another, succeed one another, and die? Cronus is the name of the
Titan who, at the beginning of the *Theogony*, frees Gaia, the
"Earth with the wide flanks,"[16] to give the world its place and to
enable successive generations to be born. Cronus opens both
space and time. Let us listen to Jean-Pierre Vernant's account:

> By castrating Uranus, on the advice and through the trickery
> of his mother, Cronus achieves a fundamental stage in the
> birth of the cosmos. He separates sky and earth. Between sky
> and earth he creates a free space. . . . Although space is freed,
> time also is transformed. As long as Uranus weighed down on
> Gaia, there were no successive generations. They remained en-
> folded in the being who had produced them. Beginning from
> the moment Uranus withdraws, the Titans can leave the ma-
> ternal fold and give birth in their turn. Thus opens a succes-
> sion of generations.[17]

This is the same Cronus (Κρόνος) who then devours his own children, with the exception of Zeus, who is saved by his mother. Thus it is not only through the effect of the wordplay between the name of Cronus and Chrónos (Χρόνος, which designates time) that the Titan, liberator of the generations, was sometimes able to be conceived as a personification of Time.

TESTS OF TIME

. . . . .

THE RETREAT OF THE ETERNAL

. . . . .

AMONG THE GREEKS, the exclusive valorization of the eternal signified the primacy of *theoria*, as associated with the contemplation of necessary and immutable truths, and the secondary place of *praxis*, which involves actions and applies to contingent things.

The philosophical privilege of pure *theoria* is a part of the Platonic and Neoplatonic tradition, whereas, for Aristotle, *praxis* and *poiesis*, the fields of action and production, are not at all unworthy of philosophy. Instead, philosophy applies to considerations of finitude and accident. Even while maintaining the hierarchy between the eternal and the temporal, it does not discount the study of becoming, that is, the "sublunar" world of beings who are born and die.[1] Here, the movements that affect the world acquire the ontological dignity denied to them by Plato.

Indeed, Platonic philosophy had saved specific and mortal beings from pure "passingness" only by recognizing their potential to "participate in" the eternal models—that is, the *Ideas*. Thus, the things of the world are copies of the *Ideas*, themselves models or paradigms. Through this *participation (méthexis)*,[2] which is a type of imitation, the fleeting aspect of things can ally itself with the eternal aspect of Ideas—the Greek word *idéa* notably signifying the permanent aspect of a thing. Platonic metaphysics thus inscribes the entire temporal world into the order of *mimesis*. The world where mortals live is the imitation of another world, "located" outside time. The reality of these eternal models explains how instead of every being's suffering death pure and simple, a certain immortality is possible in the tangible world. In the temporal world, repetition is the multiplication of copies of the same eternal paradigm (a little like events that are supposed to repeat atemporal mythic models in traditional societies).

Today, however, the recognition of the world's instability, including that of the species themselves, makes the idea of a reality of transcendent, eternal models absurd in our eyes. If nothing in the world displays permanence or identically repeats itself any longer, then the structure of imitation and the existence of archetypes lose their necessity. The relationship between model and copy was justified only in a hierarchy between eternal realities and temporal things pathetically aspiring to the perfection of their models.

The ephemeral can hope to manifest a bit of truth by participating in the immutable, imitating it, repeating it, letting itself be more or less haunted by it. But if it appears that only the ephemeral exists, truth slips away with the loss of all permanence, and ontology cuts its ties with the eternal, in other words, with the divine—or the ancient idea of the divine. Aristotle marks the moment of this break in philosophy by placing *mimesis* back into the world itself. The problem will no longer be one of participating but one of engendering.

The modern awareness of passage and the retreat of the eternal open thought to temporality and history. Nevertheless, it does not preclude all desire for what lasts. Life tends spontaneously toward growth and endurance, as Nietzsche wrote, whose thinking descends from anti-Platonism.[3] If being is only movement and thus time, the old desire for eternity can turn into only the desire for time, the desire for perseverance or for return, the power to resist death. It is because they know they are mortal that humans seek means to immortalize themselves by creating works more lasting that they are or by giving life to beings who will survive them. The choice of fecundity, like that of works, expresses a desire to *survive* that is foreign to those who believe they have access to eternity. The way in which we now devote ourselves passionately to life and youth is evidence of the *retreat of the eternal* but also of a lesser ambition to survive through the other, through generation, transmission, or works.

Aristotle, a Modern

In considering the world of beings *becoming*, Aristotle goes beyond the rigid dualism that opposes the intelligible to the sensible and the eternal to the temporal. What is more, these pairs of opposites are absolute accomplices, since the idea (the intelligible reality) is a *permanent* form. Not subject to change, it is the persistence of a presence outside time. Pure ideality has always responded to the need for a present that nothing can affect or erode, a presence sheltered from all movement.

With regard to our subject here, what makes Aristotle a modern thinker is his having removed the status of copy from the things of the tangible world even while recognizing in them a certain *contingency* not found in the celestial world. Indeed, composed of "matter" and of "form" or essence,[4] the beings of the world, even natural beings, are neither absolutely contingent nor *absolutely necessary*. Form ought to give them the principle of their being, that is, to achieve their purpose, but their mixed nature makes them fragile, and from there, Aristotelian teleology reveals itself to be *approximate*. Living beings, who are subject to generation and then corruption, are the fruit of a genesis through whose course each being realizes its own end. But the way in which beings gradually achieve their essence and attain their end remains uncertain, because material reality introduces a share of uncertainty. Accidents *can always* happen and either add to the essential or cause the essential not to be realized. Thus, becoming is not subject to an infallible program, a strict teleology, as the generation of a living being seemed to require. In being *separated from itself by time*, the evolving being does not always achieve its destination. Subject to generation and corruption, living itself already has a history. Furthermore, this history gives way to the uncertain. The existence of beings as they evolve is a matter, in varying proportions, of necessity and chance.

Thus, even if they form a strict hierarchy, the heterogeneity of the two principles, material and formal, causes a certain number of disturbances. For example, the "form" of a living being may be altered by the matter. In the worst cases, this alteration can result in the birth of monsters. Natural beings also may not fully achieve the essence of their species, as is the case with females in the animal kingdom, because they are not themselves capable of engendering, which is nevertheless an essential property of the species, although the privilege of the males alone. In this sense, the female is a "disfigured male" (*pèròma*) incomplete, abnormal, maimed), and everything takes place as if she were an accident or a deviation of nature. On this ignorance (or this denial) of the female role in procreation is constructed an androcentric conception of the species.[5] At the same time, as a foster home for the semen, the female is necessary for reproduction, thus—and this is the paradox—she is a *necessary accident*. With the female, according to Aristotle, nature deviates from itself, but it cannot do without this deviation.

Among the beings subject to generation and corruption, "made" things are more subject to accident than other things are.

Action (*praxis*) and production (*poiesis*) are faced with a contingent reality: they involve things that could be other than what they are. In these areas, where man attempts to achieve his own ends, the teleological order is clearly more approximate than it is in the natural order, and accident plays a role, just as one must include it in the description of the arts. Therefore, according to Aristotle, art is fond of fortune (*tuchè*, good luck). Indeed, art is measured by the results, by the value of a product or a work, and not by the artist's frame of mind. Thus, the artist can obtain good results through chance, without knowing why he has obtained them and without those results necessarily conforming to the end he had in mind. Therefore, there is good luck and bad luck in the execution of projects and works, and *poiesis* , unlike ethics, does not rule out chance.[6]

Of course, rule still dominates chance. One should not abandon goals or count on luck, as our contemporaries do. It remains true that as soon as accident becomes a permanent possibility, history ceases to be programmable and predictable. The time of *praxis*, like that of *poiesis*, can no longer be simply that interval separating the potential being from its achievement, that is, its end. It becomes a factor in all accidents, in all the unforeseeable, in all unexpected detours. "It is by accident that one arrives at Aegina when one did not depart with the intention of going there, but was driven there by a storm or taken by pirates."[7] Maybe in the end, one will find oneself happy to be at Aegina? Lucky or unlucky, the voyage of mortals does not necessarily take them where they would like to go.

By considering beings to be composed hierarchically of matter and form, Aristotelian philosophy established the principles for teleological thinking. But with the heterogeneity of being that these principles imply, with the inclusion of accident in ontology, Aristotelian philosophy also allows for the subversion of its own teleology. Aristotle recognized in nature, and even more in the arts and in actions, a joining of necessity and accident that expresses the independence of the temporal being in relationship to the eternal. He knew how to separate knowledge of this sublunar world from what applies to the eternal divine. No longer, by right, can anything be called eternal, immutable, or absolutely necessary in the world of mortals. This separation implies the emancipation of ontology in relationship to theology, of mortal in relationship to gods, and of philosophy in relationship to religion. The gods will be able to return, no doubt, and they will even return often, with the nostalgic *pathos* by which we recognize them, but thinking about finitude will have been inaugurated by Aristotle, the first philosopher to liberate thought from the weight of the eternal.

By examining metaphysical purity and the separation of the two worlds (the sensible and the intelligible, the temporal and the eternal)—but also of the two sexes—Aristotle plunged philosophy into the embrace of time, of the mixed, and of the heterogeneous. But the deconstruction of Platonic dualism and the difficulty of thinking about mixity still shape contemporary thought.

MOVEMENT

. . . . .

THE THINKING about time and the experience of time vary—but
we cannot say that they vary "in time" without immediately imagining a time capable of containing a history of time. Now, if there
is no history of all histories, if all history is a way of structuring
the experience of time, there also is not a universal temporality
with which we can compare or reduce all ways of experiencing
and of thinking about time. The "events"—whatever they may
be—to which we secretly or collectively refer, are the materials
with which all temporal architecture is constructed and, already,
the most ordinary experience of time. Awareness of time is neither
pure nor originary, and it cannot be separated from the empirical
contents that structure it.

By its very principle, then, our starting point is the opposite of
Kantian analysis, which attempts to extricate the concept of time
from all experience. Would the experience of time be possible if we
were not first put to the test by a certain change or, in other words,
certain events? However slight (the most minute perception is

enough), *movement* introduces that *difference* without which no *succession* could be grasped, even if it were conceivable. Any perceptible phenomenon manifesting a difference, a discrepancy, or a variation (for example, visible or audible movement) is a movement. Without such a movement, the consciousness would have no proof, no experience, of a duration, either before or after. Time is not an empty form, existing independently from any event, that clocks supposedly can indicate and that events can "fill."

Time as an *empty* or abstract order, a pure concept independent of all sensory perception, did not appear as a basic fact but as the result of philosophical elaboration. The latter would not be possible without the originary evidence of time as, first of all, a biological experience and a social institution dependent on conventions and technical constructions.

The shared experience of time offers proof of both repetition and the irreversible unique. The particular processes establishing the irreversibility of the temporal order are generation and corruption. We experience respiration, sleep and wakefulness, growth and aging, and, at the "same time," the return of the seasons, of day and night. The experience of the *regular* return of the same movement—from which are constructed conventional rhythms and more and more sophisticated temporal architectures—contrasts with the experience of a singular existence that undergoes multiple transformations and passes once and forever. It is a pathetic contrast making us aspire to long-lastingness and repetition, if not to eternity.

Time could not have been conceived philosophically as a pure or "empty" form if it had not first been technically constructed and measured. As Aristotle explains in his *Physics*, there is no time without movement or change, and it is in perceiving movement that we perceive time.[1]

To take up a question within the framework of this essay that runs through the entire history of philosophical thought and that fills whole libraries can be done only by limiting my intentions in advance. I will confine myself here to comparing two classical philosophical concepts that conflict with regard to the role of experience in the philosophical consideration of time: Kant's position, which tries to exclude time from experience in order to define it as an a priori form of sensibility, and Aristotle's position, which locates temporality as a point of interference between the soul and movement—we would say between the subjective and the objective—and inscribes the possibility of time within *the experience of movement*. In this way, Aristotle's text is more decisive and more modern than those later ones that developed sometimes realistic and sometimes idealistic ideas about time against which contemporaries would have to struggle.[2]

Kant: Time as an a Priori Form

Can we think about time by neutralizing experience? According to the Kantian conception, "Time is not an empirical concept that derives from some experience or another."[3] The impossibility of conceiving some object outside a spatial or temporal situation—in other words, the fact that for us, each thing is necessarily organized in space and in time—led Kant to consider these "forms" as belonging to the receptivity of the subjects themselves and not to the objects. The representation of space also is provided to us a priori, serving as a foundation, that is, as the condition by which an experience of phenomena is made possible. "Space is not an empirical concept that has been drawn from external experiences."[4] Kant explains, "One can never imagine that there is no space, although one can easily think there are no objects in space."[5] An analogous explanation for time is that the order of succession or of simultaneity is not provided by experience but serves as a foundation for perception: "One cannot exclude time itself in relation to phenomena in general, although one can very easily disregard phenomena within time."[6] This alleged possibility for thought—being able to think of time (or space) by setting aside phenomena—is not at all self-evident, even though it has become a commonplace in philosophical teaching. It is an essential element in the metaphysical exposition of the concepts of space and time, that is, in the definition of these two representations as a priori forms of sensibility. Thus, Kantian critical philosophy consigns time to pure interiority; it is the "form of the internal sense," as if that form could exist autonomously without the test of movement.

Things get complicated, however, if we consider that although Kant established the notion of an a priori form of sensibility, he did not say that these forms, provided to the subject, were immediately knowable. The subject can discover them only if he already has had an opportunity to *coordinate his sensations*. The principle of coordinating phenomena (according to the order of space and time) would thus be provided a priori (before all experience), but it will become knowable only if an opportunity arises for putting it into practice, for applying it to sensations. These sensations, however, are necessarily empirical in origin, which is why Roger Verneaux stresses, with good reason, that although they are a priori, the concepts of space and time are *acquired, not innate*.[7] They would not be knowable directly, outside all experience. If we accept the existence of time as an a priori form of sensibility, the temporal coordination of phenomena has no less place *in experience* over the course of experience.

Thus, time as a form is accessible to consciousness only if that form is applied; it is revealed only through its application (*Anwendung*). *Thus the intuition of succession is not pure*; it is possible only if phenomena are actually provided to perception. Thus Kant's efforts to exclude time from all experience lose much of their impact. If the order of time cannot appear to consciousness before any experience, what ensures that this order is truly provided a priori and is not the product of a *second* abstraction?

What rules out the *formation* of forms, involving from the outset the activity and passivity of the consciousness? Whether time is, finally, an a priori form remains a question if this hypothetical form is empty and if it remains unknowable as long as it is not *applied* to perceptions. The Kantian assertion according to which we can "very easily disregard phenomena within time" loses its methodological value, since this operation can be carried out only a posteriori, when the sensibility has *already* had the opportunity to *be applied*, experientially, to the perceptible facts. A consciousness deprived of all sensation, which would not be affected by any movement, would have no representation of either time or space. Enfolding time into the transcendental sphere leads to isolating a purely subjective interiority, on the one hand, and to ignoring the temporality of the world, on the other, as if the subject tacked a temporal order over factual data not belonging to time. This dualistic way of thinking obscures the most difficult question, which is precisely that of the relationship between the temporality of thought (its flow, its perpetual distance from itself) and the temporality of things in the world (generation and corruption, irreversibility, relation of cause to effect). By postulating a spatial and temporal "framework" separable from events, the Kantian method resembles Newtonian physics, according to which time is theoretically reversible, neither destroying nor creating.

By describing time as an autoaffection of the consciousness alone, harking back to Saint Augustine's *distentio animi*,[8] Husserl overcame the opposition of the subject's activity and passivity in the composition of time. But like Kant, Husserl did not want to renounce the hypothesis of an ultimate foundation for time, which he located in the direction of a transcendental subject deeper than the empirical I. Ultimately, this transcendental subject should be outside time to be able to "constitute" time. The author of *Lessons for a Phenomenology of the Intimate Consciousness of Time*[9] cannot abandon the neo-Kantian principle according to which conceiving of the subject is conceiving of the power of constructing or constituting. But what about the idea of autoaffection, which helps illuminate the temporality of the subject or, let us say, of thinking existence: can it ever be pure? With regard to thought, isn't it immediately linked to the possibility of being affected—and thus "altered," touched by the other (or by the "has been")? The alteration of consciousness, the way it can be distanced from itself, must already include a share of otherness. But if we cannot rule out the otherness of temporality, time will resist transcendental reduction; that is very much the sense of Merleau-Ponty's and Derrida's readings of Husserl, it seems to me.[10] One cannot consider time by suspending or "neutralizing" all experience, that is, all proof of the other.

The Kantian opposition between time, an a priori form of sensibility, and the material provided to the intuition rules out in advance any reflection on the conventional and artificial nature of time. Everything occurs here as if "phenomena" necessarily came to line up in the formal subjective order of succession, whereas that order is itself conceived a priori, independent of any seizure of a movement. By trying to establish an absolute autonomy, a *purity* of forms in relation to the materiality of the content, Kantian thought reduces time to a transcendental ideality—a pure, abstract form of succession or simultaneity. But as I have tried to suggest, temporality can never be grasped in its pure state: it already appears structured or "contaminated" by the empirical facts that fill it or articulate it.

Thus the question of time cannot be restricted to the pure, autonomous sphere of the transcendental subject—whether Kantian or Husserlian. The metaphysical passion for purity and autonomy, the pursuit of a simple origin, runs up against temporality and cannot be restored to a pure activity.

Moreover, transcendental analysis has the effect of separating what belongs to subjective temporality (and is a matter of metaphysics) from what concerns objective temporality, in other words, history, the field of empirical facts. Thus, historicity and temporality belong to autonomous fields as if the experience of history were independent of the test of time and thinking about time foreign to history. By putting the transcendental subject under the protection of the empirical, Kantian thought removes it from occurrence and history. But the Kantian concept of time is only one of the philosophical figures offered by the history of time. This figure is the philosophical and subjective counterpart to time as it is constructed by clocks: a universal ticktock that conditions all possible occurrence. Kant's time claims the same universality and the same homogeneity as the time of chronometers, but removed from the real, it is no more than a subjective framework, incapable of serving as base for the irreversibility of time.

In this context, some strictly heterogeneous territories emerge: the one of transcendental facts, which is a matter for philosophical "critique," and the one of empirical facts, treated by various sciences, among which is history, its object being precisely a field of empirical events. The philosophical concern for separating the formal from the material and tracing the boundary between the transcendental and the empirical has the notable effect of removing philosophy from history—but also of knocking off balance the empirical facts in a field deserted by reason. That is undoubtedly why Kant himself yielded to prejudices and succumbed to rumors when he treated empirical matters (for example, in the areas of anthropology and geography). As empirical facts, the historical conditions for thought are disqualified philosophically, whereas philosophy looks back to history only to hypothesize a natural teleology.

Generally, everything takes place as though Kantian philosophy proceeded by removing the "contents" from the concept, by trying to consider time without history, the moral without the good, and the aesthetic without the beautiful. Never has thinking been so emptied of its concrete contents in order to retain only its abstract forms. This formalism thus considers practice to be application: to act is always to apply—to apply a form or to apply a law that, moreover, must be provided outside all empirical consideration. Experience itself is thought of as the application of forms to a given, leaving to the subject the ultimate "mastery" over an encounter that cannot fundamentally affect or harm him.

Aristotle: Time as the Number of Movement

Kantian thinking about time seems less illuminating and less modern than Aristotle's, which instead tries to show how the experience of time cannot be separated from the experience of movement. According to the author of *Physics*, there is indeed a reciprocal relationship between time and movement, each being the measure of the other. One is the *number* of the other: "Not only do we measure movement by time, but also time by movement."[11] All duration is the product of an operation of measurement.

I will return to the Aristotelian text. But first, let us recall that the idea of time includes two essential dimensions: continuity and succession. Time seems to be a continuous order that nothing can interrupt. According to this order, events are placed in relationship to one another according to before and after and are compared with one another as magnitudes irreducible in space.

If two runners cover the same distance, from A to B, and if they take off at the same moment, an observer can compare their two movements. He can also compare them with another movement taken as a unit of measurement (for example, with the help of an hourglass) and establish a quantitative relationship between them called the *duration*. A witness located at target point B will be able to say which of the two arrives before the other: it is only through the eyes of the observer that the runners will be able to arrive somewhere, that is, to constitute two successive or simultaneous events. One "event" must happen somewhere to someone in order to be put in relationship to another event and for a chronology to be established.[12] The witness does not only observe; he says also who arrived first. He describes, he recounts. Here we have some indication of the grounds for a link between speech and memory, speech and the consciousness of time. The movement or the event constitutes the objective and empirical condition of time, whereas the observer or the witness—Aristotle says the "soul"—constitutes its subjective condition.

Insofar as time seems to flow "proportionately to movement," it cannot be perceived as continuous, according to Aristotle, if there is no reference to a movement itself continuous, like that of "the sphere,"[13] the sun (or the artificial mechanism of clocks). The order of the succession or the duration cannot be provided outside experience because it is necessary that movements come to articulate the repetitions or ruptures according to which an observer measures duration or defines before and after.

With Aristotle, the idea of time, like the idea of succession, is not possible without movements that allow us to distinguish successive moments, that is, a temporal differentiation. The temporal distinction of before and after, of anterior and posterior, takes place only if the soul perceives, outside or within itself, some change. In this sense, the test of movement is a condition for the test of time.

Since time *seems* to flow "proportionately to movement," we can measure it with the help of regular movements. To be more exact—and this is why Aristotle says that time "seems" to flow—we can use or create these movements to compare them with other movements (whose "duration" is thus fixed). That is what the ancients did with the hourglass, whereas Galileo used the water clock, the clepsydra, comparing it with the "time" it took a marble to roll down one part of an inclined plane. But duration is nothing more than the interval demarcated by such and such a movement.

For example, when we say of a voyage that it lasted three days, we think we have measured a movement (the voyage) by a time (three days), as if a day were a unit of time distinct from movement. But a day is a reference or an indicator of time only because it is a unit of movement that naturally repeats itself (the interval between two nights). We relate the continuous, regular movement of the sun to another movement. The regular interval serves as a unit to measure an irregular movement. This is why we can refer to the phases of the moon or the return of the seasons. The periodic return of the same occurrence (natural or artificial) allows observers to define by convention or to construct a periodicity or a rhythm. Marks, traces, repetitive differential traits, are enough for constructing sequences. The expression "temporal architecture"[14] is particularly appropriate to conveying the idea that time is neither an objective reality nor an inherent psychological fact but an order dependent on a chronometric operation, as simple as it may be. Still, this operation must not make time into a fetishism, because chronometry—whatever the system used—does not measure a time existing elsewhere; it gives it a configuration, it constructs a calendar, without which the temporal order does not appear. In the same way, it is the establishment of a periodic order that allows future dates to be indicated. Without the technical construction of a movement that recurs, that comes about because it comes back, how could we anticipate the possibility of a *to come*? Paradoxically, it is the test of repetition that "programs" a potential future.

Even if the unit of time is always provided by a movement, time and movement are not identical. We could say that time expresses the commensurability of movements. The observer calls the number shared by two movements *time*. If time is not identical to movement, it is because it is built on the distinction between the movement that measures and the movement that is measured. For the first, only the repetitive dimension is considered (an interval that repeats itself identically); for the second, the particular, concrete aspect is considered. For example, a day is *identical to a day* as the interval between two nights (the measuring movement), whereas each day is *different from the one before* by reason of the particular events that occur and are neither regular or uniform (measured movement). The distinction between the measuring movement and the measured movement does not allow the characteristics of the first to be applied to the second. Thus Aristotle denounced the idea, current in his time, that "human affairs form a circle." It must not be said that history is cyclical on the pretext that all movements are measured with the help of the "uniform circular transport," that is, the movement of the sphere.[15] This is because the movements of the world, like generation and corruption, are not themselves circular; they do not recur identically. Time becomes apparent only through its measurement; it seems to be circular, but this is only an effect of the techniques of measurement and the regular movements they use.

If uniform circular movement allows the duration of other movements to be evaluated, it does not clarify the irreversibility of the relationship between the before and after, essential to the test of time. Rather, it is much more the singular movements—those marking a change, a rupture, or the relationship of cause to consequence—that give occurrences in the world their irreversibility and thus their chronological order. The irreversibility of time is attested to in physics by the second principle of thermodynamics regarding the degradation of energy, as well as by the Joseph Fourier's equation for heat, according to which heat can circulate only toward cold and not in the other direction. Even Einstein, who hoped to eliminate irreversibility from physics, finally maintained that he did not believe it was possible to "telegraph to one's past."[16] Here again, it is the test of the event that temporality undergoes. With its determinations—regular or irregular, identical to itself or different, continuous or discontinuous—movement conditions the test of duration and of succession. It is movement that permits chronology and chronometry. Thus it is the empirical nature of rhythms and histories that gives time its form and not time that gives history its form.

This does not mean that histories are provided complete and as is. Like history, chronology also is constructed to a large degree. Again, it is to Aristotle that we owe the theorization of history in the broader sense as poetic *composition*. A history exists only through the account or the representation given to it by the poet who, unlike the simple chronicler, composes the facts to construct a whole or a system with a beginning, middle, and end. Thus in a tragedy, the history (the *muthos*: story, plot, or fable) is the whole of the actions invented by the author. The poetic arrangement of facts, what Paul Ricoeur calls the "*mise en intrigue*,"[17] is more rational than their actual succession. For Aristotle, this is why poetry is more philosophical and more universal than history (as simple chronology). Shaped and composed in this way, history constitutes the subject of dramatic tragedy, but with its demands for logic, it will become the model for all narrative (in the broader sense of narrative and dramatic composition). In other words, history, as the poetic imitation of contingent actions to which art gives a necessary order, is constructed. Whether it is a matter of fiction or "historical" narrative, all history is dependent on poetic composition. From mythological accounts to literary or historical narratives, from popular stories to those biographies each person tells himself, all history is a configuration of time and not a simple inscription of facts in time.

A Heartbeat

Any rhythm can provide a unit of time (for example, the pulse). Any regular movement can be used to construct a unit of movement and time. These units remained approximate as long as instruments could not guarantee the perfect regularity that, today, adds to the illusion of pure time. The clock became a kind of indication, a visible sign of the invisible beat of a time that "would pass."

But there is no passing and no beat other than that of things and beings and, first of all, of the rhythm of life: a heartbeat, regular breathing, an appetite that returns, the alternation between sleep and wakefulness. Why should thought—and how could it?—remove itself from the perceptible movements of its own bodily existence? It experiences them first. It can try to conceive them but not to transcend them with a leap into who knows what disembodied interiority. From the outset, biology is rhythmic, that is, temporal, made up of repetitive physical events like sleep or irreversible ones like growth and aging. Still today, the Aristotelian concepts of "generation" and "corruption" name the real foundations for the *test of time*. Breathing puts conscious existence to the test of an innate rhythm that all by itself would be enough to provide consciousness with the opportunity to experience its own temporality. Doesn't the permanent need to *catch one's breath* provide the primary example of a life that can be maintained only through a perpetual movement of exchange with the outside, in an ever repeating interval? The metabolic systems are our physical temporizations. The body offers consciousness its first movements, its primary music, its primary *tempo*.

But if this time depends on the occurrence of a rhythm, it gives itself over to an observer or a "soul." There would be no time, Aristotle insists, if there were no soul to measure movement. The subjective aspect of time forbids us to think of it as only an "external" empirical fact. Conversely, as we have seen, the movement must be *given* to the observer, a movement that he plays no part in creating and that can "exist without the soul" perfectly well. Thus the soul constructs time *with* movement, but it does not construct the movement itself. Time is neither objective nor subjective; it is the result of the encounter between the soul that "numbers" and the movement that is "numbered." Dominique Jani-caud remains faithful to this primary and powerful Aristotelian approach to time when he writes, "Chronos is never 'pure': it aris-es only because we display it, because we take measure of it."[18]

Therefore, the empirical part of the test of time, which de-pends on movements that we relate to one another (those that provide the *tempo* and those that are measured), should end the search for temporality in the direction of a transcendental subject or a pure interiority.

The Clock Radio: The Takeover of the Clock

Let us leave *Physics* to note that in its objective reality, movement is also the condition for the possibility of a common experience and a shared time. Time is not a private measure but the product of human conventions.

Every society establishes reference points for counting cycles and measuring duration. Shared time is inseparable from a convention-al social architecture and the technical means belonging to that ar-chitecture. Thus it must also be described as an *institution* depend-ent on the principal powers—religious, political, and economic, each of which imposes its own temporality with the help of techni-cal and legally appropriate instruments. It is not a matter, of course, of simple reference points: time is given a rhythm by cere-monies, rites, institutions, and laws (for example, determining work time). It also is articulated with the help of material tools for communication, telecommunication, and transport, which are so many "time machines." Today, the universal clocks are the audio-visual media, and the *clock radio* is the object that best represents the takeover, the makeover, of the clock. Indeed, this object is not a simple means for being waked up by music or with the morning news; it is the concrete sign that we live *in the time of the radio, in the time of the media,* and their programs.

Time, mediatized and universalized, imposes on our lives the time of information, in the same way that others lived according to the rhythm of the sun, the seasons, the needs of the harvest, the hunt, or the herd, and all the tasks that imposed their rhythms on humans.

Thus, we cannot speak of *the* time, as if it were homogeneous, unifiable by a single measure and a single history. There are different systems of temporality (responding to the *tempos* of various events), just as there are different systems of historicity.

For the ancient Greeks, time expressed a relationship, established by mortals, between the finite and the infinite, between a certain disorder in the sublunar world and the divine, immutable order of the heavens. Today, we are no longer dealing with anything other than an entirely constructed time. Technology has replaced the gods, that is, the heavens. This might lead us to believe that we have become the masters of time, if death didn't remind us that our days are numbered—and if each successive generation did not have to undergo again the test of growth and decline. The order of time is not offered to thought as an empty form, but very much as the law of generation by which births and deaths overlap. This is why there cannot be a continuous history or a single time.

UN PASSEUR DE TEMPS:
WALTER BENJAMIN

. . . . .

New thinking on history and a novel approach to time appeared with the writings of Walter Benjamin. It was in thinking of him, in following this stroller step by step through Parisian passageways, that the expression *passeur de temps* came to me. The author of the *Book of Passages* (*Das Passagen-Werk*),[1] an unfinished text on Paris, really does offer us a singular experience of time through his strolls. This expression, *passeur de temps*—which Benjamin himself does not use—is as impossible in German as it is in English. It does not exist in French either, but our language at least allows for its form through allusion to the expression *passer le temps*, "to pass time," and by the proximity of *passage*, "passage," and *passeur*, "ferryman."

"To pass time" signifies waste, a gratuitous way of existing without using time effectively, as a stroller does. But this meaning is not apparently related to that of *passeur*, a kind of ferryman who helps passengers *pass* from one shore of a river to the other or from one side of a mountain to the other. Our *passeur de temps* evokes these two meanings: he is open to time without trying to master it, and he is available for passage, for opening a passage from one time to another in letting himself be attracted by traces—traces of the past in the city, written traces in books. He is a *witness*, a passive observer, without whom time would not exist. And because he is both active and passive at the same time, the "passer" is also the one *by (means of) whom* something passes, he himself is the "place" of the passage. Finally, he is the impossible contemporary of himself or of *his time*, inhabiting a period in which each person keenly experiences passage.

We cannot simply see time pass: it passes *by (means of) us*. The past traverses us and comes to haunt the present in such a way that no present, no moment, no epoch, can be homogeneous. This jeopardizes the possibility of opposing the past to a present that would now be *our own*. Moreover, the notion of epoch, already problematic, now runs up against the instability of the "modern" world. If that world changes at an accelerated pace, it no longer constitutes *a* world. If we no longer have a single world, but many, if everything is transformed very quickly—although at different speeds—while the past continues to appear to us through its traces, perhaps we can no longer experience our belonging to an epoch, however "modern"?

Time traversed the nineteenth-century Parisian stroller without letting him establish himself in his own epoch, because in that century of triumphant progress, things were already changing too quickly. The Parisian galleries would provide that stroller-reader, Walter Benjamin, with a singular experience of the "passage" of time.

Strolling in Paris

Let us follow our "passer of time" for a moment and see what Paris will reveal to him. The city first gives itself over to Walter

Benjamin, and he gives it to us in his strange book as a space to *experience* and not as an object to *know*. We usually think of going from experience to knowledge, and not vice versa. In this sense, the experience by which something is given to perception is destined to be transformed into knowing, that is, into knowledge, by taking on a discursive, conceptual form. Knowing thus *translates* the experience that is obliterated by it. In this way the encounter with the thing is replaced by a thought or by the words that define it. The experience that engenders such knowledge is called *Erfahrung* in German.

This is not the kind of experience that the Benjaminian stroller seeks in his walks. This "passer" who wanders through the streets, through the passageways, and also through the pages of the texts he reads is not concerned about developing knowledge: he opens himself to *living* the experiences; he is in search of a *lived* experience, what is called *Erlebnis* in German. This is the kind of experience that touches us, tests us, and traverses us. It is sought *for itself* and not simply as a *means of knowing*. Just as knowledge can be nurtured by experience, experience can be nurtured by knowledge. Paris plunges the walker into an "anamnesic drunkenness," not only finding his nourishment in what he encounters along his path and what is "perceptible to sight," but also seizing inert knowledge and transforming it into something lived, that is, into "experience." Consider the approach of Aby Warburg, the founder of iconology, whose passion for images led well beyond erudition:

> The whole meaning of the trip to New Mexico that revealed itself to Warburg in the almost chance assembly of a text and an image is reduced to transforming the experience into a document and, inversely, of making the document a place for experience—or adventure—by returning to the world using the paths that begin from the space defined by knowledge.[2]

Like Benjamin, Warburg traveled between the world of the living and the world of the dead, between real-life adventures and bookish knowledge. Georges Bataille was inspired by Nietzsche for the same reason, because his philosophy "had for its goal not knowledge but, without separating the two, life, the *extreme*, in a word, experience itself."[3]

What happens to the Parisian stroller? To be exact: time. He experiences not only a present but also a past. The idea seems paradoxical: how can the past *happen*? Only the present seems capable of being the object of experience. It is said of historians that they cannot experience their subject, the past, and that they are reduced to working with *traces*. That is both accurate and false at the same time: the historian works very much with traces, but his subject is history, that is, not a present, a past, or a *past present*. History is an object that must be constructed, articulated, beginning with scattered traces. These compositions neither produce nor reproduce a past or present, since at the time they come about, the facts do not yet constitute a history. This history happens in a certain weave of traces, in a text or an account—and nowhere else.

But the stroller has no ambition to be a historian: strictly speaking, he constructs no account—even if he lets a text take form. He does not even reconstruct a memory if the latter assumes an appropriation of the past. The historian takes possession of the past by interpreting traces, whereas the trace of the past *happens* to the stroller and takes possession of him. Let us not claim, however, that nothing *happens* to the historian; undoubtedly his desire also involves an anticipation, a curiosity with regard to what will come to him from the past, what he will discover in the shadows and encounter. There is often a stroller at the heart of each historian, a part of him that is trying to let himself be touched by the traces.[4]

The experience of the city does not offer knowledge or an appropriation of the past but, rather, a test of strangeness. The past to which the stroller relates is not a past that would earlier have been present to him and now returns to him. It is a past that is absolutely not *his own*: "The street leads to a bygone past. For him, each street slopes downhill ... and leads into a past that can be all the more entrancing *because it is not his own past*, his *private* past."[5] No return leads him to a point in his own past—in other words, no memory is involved. The bygone past is an "absolute" past, that is, separate, secret, strange.

For a past where we have never been, *reappropriation* is not possible; how could I make present to myself a past that has never been mine? I am excluded from it and remain so. But isn't it exactly in this feeling of exclusion that the relationship to the past—always—opens? The experience of a past that has never been mine, as neither a moment lived nor an epoch, is not a voyage into time during which I could transport myself, unchanged, intact, yonder, to pass from now to formerly and inhabit a former time. The experience of the past is one of a world *without me*, a world from which I am absent, its echo alone reaching me.

For the Parisian "passer," the past comes to resonate in the present, and the present is a way to the past. With the *aura*, it is the distant that reaches me and makes itself "master of me"; with the *trace*, it is the near, the *here* and the *now*, that leads me to the distant. In each case, the times intersect in me, with no possible synthesis. The near seems inhabited by the distant, and the trace is excluded from the simple present, letting the past show through its surface. The experience of the past, Benjamin suggests, is always that of a hollow, a hole in the apparent fullness of the present—without letting one say if it is the past or the present that seems anachronistic.

My "own" past, that is, the part of existence that henceforth escapes my grasp, hardly excludes me less than does the past in general. It is the indication of a *too late* and a *never again*. It designates less a chronologically definable whole than it involves all the events of my life, distant or close, that I can no longer change. Basically, it is the whole of what, in my life, no longer has any future.

Thus the past seems less a question of coming before than of being old. It evokes things that no longer have *currency*, that no longer circulate, their movement or action having stopped. Like an old coin or a dead language, the things of the past have fallen out of use, and it is not up to us to make them circulate again, because the test of time is always firmly bound to the irreversible movements of a world that we inhabit with others.

If the past is the field of our powerlessness, the present is the possibility for a lasting state or movement. The grammatical use of the present tense demonstrates that the present does not indicate the instant but an *unfinished* event, a now that lasts. "I live on such-and-such street," we say, and there is no need to specify for how long (a day or years). The time for a task, the time for lunch or a conversation, are in the present tense as long as they are not over irreversibly. The use of the present does not evoke a precise moment, and even less a conventional chronometric unit (for example, a second), but the relative duration of a certain movement, long or short. Far from being the flash of an instant, my present is, instead, made up of a certain "surface" or layer or, rather, a superimposition of *layers of time* of different widths, according to the different durations of the "movements" of my life.

Conversely, the instant marks the *border* of a layer of time; it is the moment when something is decided, the critical, vertical moment, the point where the road splits, the extremity of a movement that is going to stop or change direction. Any instant is crucial, any instant is decisive, or it is not *the instant*. It interrupts a lasting state or movement; it makes one layer of time slip into the past and opens another one.

Wasting Time

For Benjamin, the possibility of experiencing the past requires certain conditions. In particular, the frame of mind for letting oneself be touched, for letting oneself be taken by the *aura*, requires a true idleness. The stroller cannot want to arrange time himself, for example, by undertaking some project or by precisely scheduling his course of action; rather, he must be available to time, *to let time pass*, to spend it without keeping count, to know how to waste it. He must give up making it his own, the time he ought to be paying attention to if he were doing something. It is as *dead* time that duration becomes palpable.

Ordinarily, it is the use of time that defines availability: my time is available (or I am available at such-and-such a time) if I have *not yet* planned how to use that time, if I can still use it for this or that occupation. It is time itself that seems available for my actions, and not I who is available to time. For the stroller, it is the other way around: he makes himself strangely available to time because he has given up using it. Such availability is not simply waiting or a kind of passiveness. He must not just "make time pass"; he must also "invite it home" (*einladen*). He must "take on time" (*laden*).[6]

But what can it mean to "take on time" if time is nothing, if it is only the relative measurement of a movement? It could be this: to accept not having time oneself, not becoming involved in the temporality of an action—thus making it possible to accommodate the event, to be open to what passes, to what takes place, and to grant things their own temporality, their own particular rhythm.

The one whose eyes follow the flight of a gull over the sea adopts the temporality of that flight; his time becomes the gull's time. The stroller's idleness is similar to the idleness of a reader or someone at a play or a movie. Each of them yields to the rhythm of a movement that is not their own. In forgetting his own movement, and thus his own time, the stroller embraces the time of things. But the gull's time is not the departing boat's time, or the rock's time emerging from the waves, or the child's time playing on the beach. In the midst of a world that passes at such different speeds, the contemplative observer *loses time*. He no longer has his own time, and he feels the absence of absolute temporality. When we leave a movie theater, we also must leave the film, and its temporality that our thoughts had so intimately embraced, to rediscover our own time and our own life. For an instant, we remain suspended between two times.

The "passer" is also the one in whom traces intersect: a weave of the city, rocks, monuments, streets, images, things seen and things read, street signs or books, stories told. The walker reads many texts at once, while each of them resonates with the others. Such bookish knowledge penetrates his present perceptions. Thus, on the rue des Martyrs, which climbs steeply behind the Notre-Dame-de-Lorette Church, the walker *knows* that in the past an additional horse was harnessed; and there at the moment he himself takes this street, the steeper climb makes itself felt in his knees. A simple bit of knowledge becomes something lived; the effort to struggle up the street becomes more felt by the anamnesis of the omnibus and horse that it used to be necessary to add. What Francis Bacon called "lettered experience" (experience transmitted through books) interferes here with a reading of the city that comes about through walking. Thus the walker's *lived* experience is traversed by a "second existence," the result of books, in such a way that the different types of experience merge and fade into one another. The *lived* experience is not in any way opposed to the *lettered* experience; each is informed and transformed by the other. Anamnesic drunkenness takes possession of the reader just as it does the walker.

Today, this drunkenness is also shared by the spectator. Because our experience of the city, like our experience in general, is, to a large extent, an *imaged* experience. The experience of images, as we will see, is incorporated into the lived experience.

An Ambivalent Modernity

The "passer" is a reader who writes, a writer who reads. The writer of *The Passages* achieves a work of collage or montage with the texts he collects, assembling the pieces and juxtaposing some of his own texts with "passages" from Baudelaire or Nadar, from Maxime Du Camp or Balzac. Here Benjamin's writing borrows new compositional techniques from the plastic arts, like cinema. The writer passes between the texts and makes us pass there, building bridges from one to the other, making original montages. Thus, he gives up a share of his "authority" to let the passages form agglomerations of writings. This new genre of book seems to imitate the city and let itself be explored like a city. Giving up on answering for all the discourse by himself, just as an architect cannot answer for the entire city, the writer of the *Passagen-Werk* does not hope to master all the effects of this *mixed* writing. Just as if it cannot comprehend the city in its totality or give it meaning, Benjamin's writing imitates the heterogeneity of the urban fabric.

Let us return again for a moment to the Parisian passageways themselves to see how they reveal an ambivalent or anachronistic figure of modernity. At the same time as it values the new, modernity discloses its singular fragility. Until then, it was especially human life that seemed brief and fragile. But while Baudelaire regrets that "the form of a city changes more quickly, alas, than the heart of a mortal,"[7] he also expresses this modern reversal: the human heart is more stable than the world in which it lives; it is more constant than a city. The Parisian stroller also witnesses this reversal: he is the witness of a world *in the process of passing*, just as a color fades; he is witnessing the very event of the city's aging. Things move away before his eyes just as landscapes grow distant under the gaze of those watching slide shows.

Through the good fortune of the French language, it is precisely the Parisian passageways from the Second Empire that offer the stroller the best experience of *passing*. The corridors with glass ceilings that run through whole blocks of buildings, as described in an 1852 guide to Paris, exemplify a city aging prematurely, a space still new and already *passé*. On the one hand, these passageways still illustrate the triumph of progress and its splendor, technical innovation, luxury, fashion, gas lighting, the abundance of merchandise. On the other hand, their speedy obsolescence transforms this audacious architecture into the simple remains of a world that is falling apart before our eyes. Thus, these galleries testify to the essential ambivalence of modernity. In supplanting gas, electricity already consigns the passageway to the past: "By suddenly flaring on, electric lights made pale the irreproachable splendor of these galleries."[8] For Benjamin, it is more a matter of a "reversal" than a decline. The image of the new already symbolizes the old. Fashion becomes old-fashioned; progress dispels progress. The jubilant modernity of the passageway topples over into obsolescence, endlessly betrayed by the present. Incapable of signifying a stable kind of novelty, opposable to a former world, it names the passing itself.

Thus, the nineteenth century only seems "modern" in making things age at an accelerated pace, in dating the world, to the point of appearing to Benjamin like a "a retirement home of child prodigies." In this regard, is our century any different? Maybe not, since we move at an even more rapid pace still.

Indeed, passage could be apprehended as the movement of a *pace*, the visible, urban pace of modernity, the very movement of what arises and occurs *in the process of passing*. This pace belongs neither to the now nor to the formerly. It takes place in the in-between—between two streets, between two times. It is never a present but an accelerated movement, a scene in which the characters seem to move too quickly, like the actors in silent movies. With film, images have, in their turn, shown us, in an even more astounding way, the world in the process of passing.

The exemplary nature of the nineteenth-century Parisian passageways is also in keeping with the undefined status of the objects found there, suspended, lost between two epochs: here a dusty wedding veil indicates a store for wedding and banquet rosettes, but "we no longer believe in them." Fancy buttons are sold for collars and shirts that no longer exist. A hodgepodge of merchandise is still offered to customers, but there again, no one really believes anymore. The passageway has not yet entered into a bygone past, and it is already no longer current. It is simply displaced, outmoded, anachronistic, as if by multiplying the rhythms, the speeds, the histories, modernity opened the impossibility of a present and established us in a world of bric-a-brac.

The Age of Objects

The charm of Benjamin's thinking lies less in theoretical constructions than in the imagination that he engages in the face of things, in his materialist reveries. He does not lead us toward ideas but toward things. The stroller makes us imagine the "life" of objects.

It is neither their origin nor their manufacturing date that defines the time of objects. Each of them enters into the past when it is outmoded, *dépassé*. Its belonging to the present or to a bygone time does not depend on its place in time but on the appearance, or not, of another object to replace it. Natural things—which have a history nevertheless, since they are transformed—are part of no epoch of human time. A mineralogist can no doubt date a simple stone in the history of the universe, but for us, it cannot be "old." It is ageless because we cannot replace it with anything.

Relatively recent objects, dating from twenty or thirty years ago, for example, like a transistor or an automobile, seem strangely *old*, whereas an ordinary piece of furniture, its use unchanged, can last a long time without being "out of synch." What does not lend itself to technical refinement, like a rustic wooden table, is not outmoded by another more recently produced object. On the contrary, age and patina give it that "antique value" so accurately described by Aloïs Riegl.[9] It is the social history of techniques and materials that sets the rhythm for the age of things and does or doesn't consign them to a bygone past.

Most objects belong to many layers of time to the extent that their different natures or uses are not all contemporary with one another. Simultaneously, they can be present, available now for a current function, and can be holdovers from another time, another context in which they developed.

Far from depending only on some interior and subjective memory, the ordinary test of time is conditioned by our relationship to objects and places. We all are the age of our objects and experience our own aging at the same time as theirs. Our relationship to others also involves things, and we feel ourselves to be the contemporaries of those who share the same material world with us. Generation gaps owe much to changes in objects and technology.

"Every man belongs to two eras,"[10] noted Valéry, opposing the slow, continuous time of the past to the surprises and discontinuities of the twentieth century. We are way beyond that. Henceforth, the eras multiply. Each area of the material or intellectual world, each institution, moves to its own rhythm at its own pace.

It is not easy to adapt to these multiple times. A human life no longer constitutes a temporal unit as it once did. It is split up by the acceleration of history and by the new fragmentation of time. When we encounter the transistor of our childhood in a museum, the formerly familiar object becomes a strange relic, offered to the amazement of new eyes and to the curiosity of historical knowledge. Thus exposed, the object, still alive in subjective memory, drags our past experience along with it into the space of the museum, that is, into history and death. The outdated object from my youth makes me feel my own age and dates me a bit myself. I do not know whether I have crossed through many epochs or whether various epochs cross through me. It seems to me that there are many worlds and many times. But maybe that is what it is to be *modern*?

The impression of anachronism that sometimes seizes us is due, moreover, to a contemporary approach to the world that henceforth comes through images: from Daguerre to digital images, the experience of time is also an imaged experience.

THE TIME OF IMAGES

. . . . .

HISTORICAL POLEMIC:
THE MODERNITY OF PHOTOGRAPHY

. . . . .

The appearance of photography marked the opening of hostilities between artistic "modernity" and technical "modernity." In the middle of the nineteenth century, artistic modernity consisted of accepting, to a certain extent, new styles of painting and writing. Technical modernity brought with it a few strange inventions, among them a process for producing images by capturing a trace of light on an appropriate medium. These images, which had no relationship to those in paintings, were unusual objects, and no one could consider them works of art—not Delacroix or Baudelaire, or many others. But maybe the problem was that the concept of art was incapable of *containing* photography.

Nevertheless, in retrospect, we can say that modernity had indeed arrived in this new possibility for making images that would not only create a new art form but also disrupt the history of other arts. Why was it that the concept of art could not open itself to this technical modernity? In what sense did modernity throw a concept like art into crisis?

The various uses of the words *modern* and *modernity* are always the indication of a historical polemic, in many senses. First of all, it is the battle that the present wages against the past insofar as the event is not a repetition of the same and something new is possible. Modernity presupposes a creative time, even if history is only the conflict between the event and the order that it destroys.[1] Thus history signifies that an event is capable of making a new situation irreversible, and thus that time becomes differentiated in particular moments.

Another source of the polemic: modernity is ambivalent, dependent on historical thought. According to whether or not it has a destination, history does not give the same meaning to the present and does not think of it in the same relationship to the future. If history has a meaning, the modernity of the present is not only what condemns the past; it is the threshold of a future that it is already capable of thinking about and anticipating. The present is situated in the middle of a history envisaged in its totality. We think we know where it comes from and where it is going, and from this destination, we deduce the present imperatives. If history is only the idea of a creative time, its ultimate work remaining unknown because it is always to come, modernity will assert itself against a past that it supplants and an "old" that it determines as such, but it necessarily will remain open and undecided. Like the present imperative, even if modernity always involves the future, even if it considers itself more than ever responsible for an indeterminate future, it has before it only a short time—a small straight line in which who knows what event will mark a bend we can no longer see beyond. Thus, the irreversibility of time and the difference between epochs can be contemplated without assuming that the course of things is oriented by a destination.

History considered from the perspective of a destination starts with the philosophy of Aristotle, beginning with the moment when nature is grasped as distinct from itself, not immediately identical to itself, separated from itself by a time that requires it to grow or be transformed, like plants or animals, in order to attain its end. This historicity of nature is still only a delayed completion, a *differing* and a *deferring* in which being meets up with and fulfills itself in identically reproducing itself, like the individual who, developing over time, achieves its own essence and becomes capable of reproducing its kind. Time is the source of the "scission" for being, but as Pierre Aubenque emphasizes, it is the possibility of both generation and corruption, growth and decay.[2] It is also the "benevolent auxiliary to thought and human action,"[3] permitting successive generations to perfect what had initially been outlined. In the domain of knowledge or the arts, everyone can, according to Aristotle, hope to add to what was left incomplete.

If thinking of time as the source of being's scission allows for the idea of progress, it is forever opening possibilities for the opposite: time that undoes, degradation, corruption, decay—another meaning of history. Thus modernity as the present phase of a historical process oriented toward its end will *sometimes* be valorized as a step toward completion, the achievement of "progress," *sometimes* as one more step toward defeat, a descent, a dismal advance. These two values for modernity are also those of "modern man," according to whether he is perceived within the historical perspective of progress or decline. With characteristic humor, Flaubert allocates between Bouvard and Pécuchet these two views of modern man and these two oversimplified conceptions of history: "Pécuchet sees the future of Humanity in black: Modern Man is diminished and has become a machine. The final anarchy of humankind. . . . Bouvard sees the future of Humanity as beautiful. Modern Man is progressing."

Note that the regression in which Pécuchet believes, with his black view of history, went hand in glove with a progressive mechanization that would erode human humanity. Accelerated technical evolution is at the heart of the two interpretations of the future just-ly evoked by Flaubert: the black and the beautiful. They are coun-terparts in that the progression and multiplication of new tech-niques can be read as *progress* and valorize "modern" man only if humanity, already considered and defined outside this technology, retains mastery over it and uses it to serve its own ends and its de-sires. Technical progress is *human* progress only if it remains the *ex-ternal* tool of man as classical humanism conceived of him. But if it threatens to require that humanity be conceived differently, to call into question humanity's relationship to nature, if it weakens the idea humanity holds of itself, then it disorients history and create the fear that modern man is lost. The two conceptions of modern man, optimistic and pessimistic, define him outside technology and independent of it—that is how they are in collusion. They diverge in the idea that technology can either serve man or ruin him.

But the problem is knowing whether we can still think of hu-manity independent of technology. Isn't this the question that a new technological culture poses, now more than ever, throwing into crisis the idea that humanity shapes itself and its art?

A War That Time Wages on the Concept

Man seems to accept or ratify history only if he can make it *his* history in advance, if he can understand the sense of it beginning with his own plan and his conscious will. What classical human-ism (through metaphysics) refuses to consider is that history can continually extend beyond the aims that man himself sets, that oc-currence—even if he is also the actor in it—can surprise him to the point of transforming him and making it hard for him to recog-nize himself. Nevertheless, it may be to such risks that history ex-poses us, in particular the history of techniques.

In the field of anthropology, André Leroi-Gourhan was able to advance the theory that technical revolutions bring with them profound changes in "humanity," both biological and behavioral, both individual and collective, and that they mark distinct stages in human history. These stages are so different that the anthropologist dares to assert: "If the parallel with the zoological world can be maintained only at the cost of paradox, it also is impossible not to consider that humanity *changes the species a bit* each time it changes both tools and institutions."[4] Focusing especially on the transformation of social relationships beginning with "the unlimited externalization of the driving force," he adds, "a nonhuman observer, remaining outside the explanations to which we've grown accustomed through history and philosophy, would distinguish the nineteenth-century man from the twentieth-century man as we distinguish the lion from the tiger, or the wolf from the dog."[5]

That is to say, with much audacity, that man must write his history by accepting his own heterogeneity and must agree to designate, under this name of man, a strange capacity for "changing the species"! This would entail recognizing a transformation of "nature" or the human essence and admitting that time implements a scission of being that is more profound than the one Aristotle conceived, more radical, too, than a scission conceived of dialectically that assumes the identity of the concept will be preserved.

This is very much the question that history poses: how to know whether it is the time of some destiny being carried out, if it has the unity of a rational evolution, that is, of the progressive realization of a plan, however hidden, either natural or human; or, rather, always interrupting any programming, if it gives way to accident, fracture, discontinuity, heterogeneity, up to and including the heterogeneity of humanity. Should we even still speak of history if the identity of the concept supposedly manifested there is threatened by it? To what degree can the old concepts survive if an event can create an absolutely new order? Either history is continuous and assumes the identity of whatever it is the history of, or it is discontinuous and signifies that the concept is transformed over time.

Thus when we speak of the history of art, taking into account the eruption of the new in its radical form, we can ask ourselves whether time lets the concept of art develop into its successive determinations (according to a dialectical conception) or whether time is not capable of "shredding" the concept of art itself. In this case, we could no longer speak of the modernity *of art* or even *in art*, in the sense of an art unchanged in concept. We would have to think of modernity—such are the stakes for these questions—as a war that time wages against the concept, like the concept's moment of crisis confronted with the sudden appearance of the new. Occurrence cannot always be inscribed into the history of the concept: taking it into account belongs to an empirical approach to history that is adopted here.

Romantic Modernity

With Baudelaire, modernity names a crisis in the classical concept of art, even while remaining dependent on a spiritualistic vision that serves as a defense against technological modernity.

Dominated by the pursuit of the beautiful ideal, the classical concept of art collides here with a world in which the city, industry, and fashion offer art their ephemeral models. Modernity is not a period of art and is not inscribed in a dialectical history; it only names the necessity, for all art, of belonging to its time. It makes no claims to progress, but it takes issue with classical thinking that does not allow time the possibility of modifying the ideal. In his 1823 *De l'imitation*,[6] Quatremère de Quincy was still faithful to Cicero in affirming that the models for art reside *for all time* in the intellect and reason. According to the classical doctrine, the ideal image, which it is art's goal to create, is never to be found in the empirical examples or models on which memory and imagination solely depend. It can be contemplated, outside all time and all place, only by the mind.

It is the timeless ideal of classicism stagnated in academicism, the ideal that believes in the endurance of models and invites only imitations of the ancients, that Baudelaire shatters with the imperative of modernity. He does not oppose the punctuality of the present to an eternal ideal; he cuts the old concept in two and affirms its duality, parallel to that of man. Art simultaneously presents the immutable and the changing, the eternal and the fleeting—what time brings and takes with it of the passing, the contingent, the circumstantial—in short, the "modern."

Thus modernity does not name a new age for art; it is only, according to the well-known expression, "half of art."[7] Better still, this new way of thinking about art in its duality or its ambiguity does not involve only the works of the moment; it presents its claim for replacing the old concept by applying retroactively to the great works of the art. All true art was modern in its time, and even if they did not know it, the ancients had already extracted "the eternal position of beauty" from their own time.

Thus, Baudelairian modernity advances a new conception that requires the work of art to relate to its time. It is in this sense that paradoxically, modernity becomes a recurring demand. It will be continually necessary to be modern, and this will never mean the same thing, apart from that requirement of a relationship with its own time. That is why the salons do not speak to us of the modern painter but of "the painter of modern life," the life from which he must extract present beauty: his mission consists of painting the beauty of the present and of making present, eternally, the beautiful.

We remain faithful here to Baudelairian thinking about modernity by privileging consideration of the ephemeral and by recognizing in it an artistic as well as a philosophic necessity. But we cannot recognize ourselves, or our times, in Baudelaire's fierce opposition to what the world offers that is absolutely new: its techniques and its industry.

Art and Technique

Romantic modernity wanted to paint its times even while conflicting with the techniques of those times and what was then called *progress*. "Poetry and progress are two ambitious men who hate each other with an instinctive hatred,"[8] wrote Baudelaire in 1859. As "the progressive domination of the material,"[9] progress has nothing to do with beauty and collides with it. The debate over photography expresses this conflict between the artistic and the technical.

Freed to some extent from the classical ideal, romantic modernity thereby also set itself up to resist the threats that modern techniques brought to bear on traditional arts. Under the criticism of photographic exactitude, the real stakes for artists meant defending the total mastery of their work, in particular, mastery over the *means* of expression that are—and must remain—techniques. The epoch's innovations did not create the conflict between the artist and techniques, but they brought it to a head.

For Baudelaire, technical progress—"steam power, electricity, and gas lighting"—is only a matter of a material order foreign to the purely spiritual order to which art aspires. Thus, a new technique can in no way rival art or transform it. At best, it can be art's "very humble servant," an exact material record at the service of the spirit, of true memory and imagination.

Nevertheless the world changes and offers the artist new models: the customs of the time, the moral standards, the passions, the style, the attitudes. The body itself changes—"each epoch has its own bearing, expression, smile"[10]—and the modern *lorette* is no longer the courtesan painted by Titian or Raphael. The myth of the natural model, with its abstract, naked universality, withdraws, giving way to the dress of the time with its styles and its fabrics. Even the faces are characterized by their period. But to emphasize "the stamp that the *time* imprints on our sensations," to agree that the artist observes and represents the ephemeral beauty of the time, to want the painter to reproduce "the sober and elegant *beauty* of the modern ship,"[11] and to abandon the complicated sails of the sixteenth century, none of that calls into question the method of representation or leads to the assumption that methods can change. This modernity demands from art images of the *modern world*, but it never considers the birth of *a modern image* of the world.

This is because the image that is born with photography and treated at first only as a rival or a servant of art must not call into question "the queen of the faculties": imagination, whereas the photographic process (optical and chemical), however many its uses, creates the possibility of producing "images" of the world that are no longer dependent on the imagination. The realization that the photograph was an image without imagination (in the old sense) often led to the attempt to prove that it could not be art. Yet the nature of the imagination itself and, beyond that, the definition of art, remained unquestioned.

A Memory of the Present

Thus, romantic modernity decided in favor of "art," as opposed to photography, again reinforcing the old disagreement between material, even mechanical, exteriority and the spiritual interiority of the imagination. As if to widen the gap between the exactitude of the photographic image—even more accurate than visual perception—and the idealized image of art, Baudelaire attempts to critique the role of perception itself in order to show that it is not fundamental to the artistic imagination: the material exactitude of photography, which fascinates the "idolatry crowd," betrays art because it betrays the soul and its dreams. Baudelaire denies photography true "exactitude": "They believe that, the madmen!"[12]

Thus it is a matter of marking the distance that separates ordinary perception from the artist's particular view or, better still, his "method," the term used with regard to the painter Constantin Guys.[13] Indeed, this method consists of drawing *from memory* and not from a model. Furthermore, it would not be a matter of a method if here memory named a simple temporary suspension from observing the model during the time of the actual drawing. Obviously, unless you are tracing, you always draw "from memory"—even in the presence of a model—since observing the model and drawing the lines are not strictly synchronous. As early as 1759, one could read in the *Mercure*, "Although having Nature present, the draftsman can nevertheless draw it only from memory, he does not at all literally copy Nature, *since he no longer sees it when he looks at his paper*. It is the image that he has retained."[14] Thus it is not necessary that the model be absent for perception to be suspended and for justifying the use of the word *memory*. But everything depends on the role that memory is granted. As with Baudelaire, memory here already evokes the need for passing through an "interior model" distinct from nature ("this is not what he copies"). This "interior model," so important to the history of art theories, is not at all necessary, however.

As with any other mimetic behavior, imitation through drawing does not need a *mental representation*. It is not because a gesture follows from an observation, with more or less delay, that something *internal* takes place between the two. Nevertheless, that is the assumption in attributing to the memory this ability to produce an image mediating between an observation and the execution of a drawing. From this derives Baudelaire's classic claim: "All good and true draftsmen draw according to the image written in their minds, and not according to nature."[15] This reference to the image "written in the mind" recalls the idealist or even the "mannerist" tradition, which separates the physical eye from the mind's eye and the *internal* drawing from the *external* drawing.[16]

Baudelaire attributes the formation of the interior image to a procedure by which the memory breaks with applied observation and achieves a perceptual synthesis. Classical authors had already asked memory to perform a task of synthesis, but then beyond the empirical models, it had to grasp an eternal idea or ideal. On the contrary, romanticism wants it to seize hold of the most fleeting thing the model offers: the momentary impression produced by the things on the mind, in short, a memory of the present.

To perform this "task," the draftsman must be quick: he must stop his observation and not lose himself in the "riot" of details that the real offers him and that paralyze him. Here memory's task is less to retain a past perception than to synthetically seize the fleeting impression at the heart of the perception itself. The synthesis does not take place in the aftermath of the perception; it must coincide with it. In connection with Corot, doesn't Baudelaire praise the painters "whose vision is synthetic and abbreviating"?

The mnemonic method does not, therefore, imply the absence of the model. It is more a method of rapid observation than a use of memory, a way of not seeing everything, of selecting impressions, and thus of *imagining the real* at the very moment of perceiving it. Nevertheless, is the synthetic regard itself enough to ensure the permanence of the impression, or does that really require something else?

Drawing, a Method of Memory

To ensure the permanence of the impression, so that memory fulfills its role, requires art, requires drawing, requires the execution that produces the image. That is very much what Baudelaire seems to indicate in the last part of "*L'Art mnémonique*," which suggests that memory and imagination take place in the execution of the work itself and not before.

This is because it is no longer the memory's quickness that can capture the impression; it is the execution. If the draftsman's model were really written "in his mind," memorized, would there be any need to hurry? It must be that the one who draws "from memory" does not retain very well the images that the memory has formed, since as Baudelaire describes it, he is so afraid of losing them that he must execute his drawings in the greatest haste. Thus, in Constantin Guys's executions we find "a drunkenness of pencil, of brushwork, almost resembling frenzy. This is the fear of not going quickly enough, of letting the phantom escape before the synthesis can be extracted from it and seized."[17]

Thus, the images with which the artist "filled" his memory were very fleeting: phantoms that escape. The synthesis was not truly performed: it was necessary to extract it, seize it, so that the mnemonic method gives way in the end to the description of a *method of execution*.

The sacrifice of details, earlier attributed to the memory—indeed even to the observation—now takes place simply through the drawing technique. The stages of a drawing produce neither the pieces nor the parts of it. The draftsman superimposes three structures in succession, each of which is only a sketch, but a perfect sketch—a light outline in pencil, then an application of washes, and finally the outline of the objects in ink. Each of the three techniques employed presents a "finished" aspect, Baudelaire stresses, as if to show that the work, like the impression produced by things on the mind, will not let itself be broken up. But the superimposition of the three processes (sketch, washes, ink) proves, rather, the reverse: each step expresses a part of the overall appearance, in such a way that the artist superimposes his techniques and adds up various views.

In the end, this focus on the artist's technique minimizes the work first attributed to the memory or the imagination. The latter is not an autonomous faculty that controls the material. It is much more the technique that produces the synthesis and, in creating an *image of the present*, retains the memory of it.

Baudelaire does not go so far as to identify the memory with the technique, always singular, of producing an image. For him, the material work remains on the order of an "execution," with all that this term implies about obedience to an order given by the mind. Nevertheless, we could suggest that the modernity of an artist like Constantin Guys, if it really has something to do with its way of offering an image of the modern world, cannot be dissociated from the fact that he invents a drawing technique. His art is in this technique, in his way of "imaging" more than imagining. The phantoms of the imagination would be nothing without the singular art that captures them. From then on, the technique could not be an *instrument*, in the sense of a servant alien to the orders given it. In *carrying out its material execution*, the drawing is more a condition of the memory—its necessary "medium"—than it is the derived expression of it.

What is at stake, then, in this change in perspective is whether the arts can be conceived outside their techniques, if the artist can neutralize them, make them into instruments, simple servants. If this is not the case, art cannot be independent of technical innovations.

Baudelairian modernity calls into question the classical concept of art, but it cannot detach itself from traditional techniques, in the wider sense of the term. Models for the work are not eternal, but the arts seem to be so.[18] Nevertheless, if memory needs the technique of drawing, how can it be forbidden from taking recourse in other techniques and other images?

To admit the possibility of such recourse would be to renounce the traditional rivalry between the spiritual and the material domains, to which Baudelaire remains deeply attached. He does not let "exterior" material reality contaminate "interior" spiritual reality; he wants to maintain as separate—and this is a classic gesture—the mind's memory that synthesizes, retains, and internalizes, and an exterior memory that has the completely material exactitude of archives. Photography can, at best, fulfill this function and be to the true artistic memory what printing or stenography is to the writer. But it is not allowed "to encroach on the domain of the impalpable and the imaginary, on all that matters only because humans give something of their soul to it."[19]

Yet photography cannot be granted this role of art's servant or auxiliary without paradox or risks. If one claims, as Delacroix did, that the mind does not embrace all that the eye offers it," why even ask photography to serve as an instrument for "remedying the errors" that the eye might make?[20] Why work from photographs, as Delacroix did, and recognize in them "the true design of nature"? The "technical" servant acquires a real power. There can be no doubt that it has already begun to encroach on "art," its master.

An Avant-Garde Spiritualism

The conflict between romanticism and technical modernity extended well beyond Baudelaire into the heart of the avant-gardist theories of twentieth-century art. It always took the form of a struggle between subjective interiority and "exteriority," especially concerning techniques. In its extreme form, it went so far as to reject any relationship between art and exteriority in general, that is, the world itself. Many artists, theoreticians of abstraction, unanimously condemned all forms of imitation in the name of a purely interior and spiritual foundation for art. Kandinsky wanted the interior spirit to sweep away the "filth of exteriority."[21] The astonishing violence of these remarks is on par with that of

other Russian spiritualists like Berdiaev or Merejkovski who re-
volted against "the futurist filth" and denounced any form of
"materialism." Even today, a philosopher like Michel Henry continues to contemplate an aesthetic culture foreign to all technology, opposed to the world of "materiality." The vibrant appeal to
spirituality serves as a defense here against technology, "blind and
foreign to human desire"[22] and always treated with a disdainful
ignorance. It is foreign to the only true creative culture, that of the
mind and of vital subjectivity, in other words, of "pure sensibility." Let us quickly skim over the "unfathomable depths" of this
interiority, over its nocturnal dimension, over its "Night" (always
with a capital N), over this *invisible* reality that art alone can reveal and that jettisons the visible world.[23] The metaphysical obsession with purity here continues to oppose pure, invisible interiority to material exteriority, showing that the romantic conflict
between art and techniques is extremely persistent.

An Image Without Imagination

Photographic technique makes this conflict explode because it
produces images and not those contemptible "useful objects" foreign to the beautiful and made by "stupid machines," according
to Rodin. In this way, photography falls into the domain of imitations and thus art. But for all that, it cannot enter this noble domain because its means are "mechanical" (today we would say
optical and chemical). In addition, the definition of art as *mimesis*, an imitation or representation of perceptible or intelligible reality, has always excluded "mechanical" production.

Thus, ever since the liberal arts were distinguished from the
mechanical arts, the fine arts have staked their claim on the spirit. Conversely, the "mechanical" names that absence of spirit in a
purely material work. The eclipsing of technique in Western
thinking, that is, in technical civilization par excellence, is gener-

ally bound up with a theoretical repression of the material production of things.

It is not a matter here of going to any extreme to include photography in the concept of art as it had been classically defined but of understanding why art—in the sense of the fine arts—could not *take in* photography. This is because in the plastic arts, *mimesis* signifies the invention of an image by the imagination. Photography was, nevertheless, considered in relationship to *the classical category of imitation*, an unsuitable category, since it essentially relies on the principle of representing an idea. By supplanting painting in many of its functions (for example, portraiture), photography was first understood in terms of a comparison between the two.

Reading Quatremère de Quincy,[24] we can indeed verify that imitation requires invention and excludes, as it always has, the servile copy. Here, imitation is organized according to the concept of repetition, and includes three forms:[25]

- The *moral imitation*, which is the inventive repetition of the object through an image "requiring of its author the resources of genius, sentiment, and imagination."
- The *copy*, which requires talent and intelligence but not invention, since it reproduces an already invented image.
- Finally, the *material imitation*, which is "the repetition of an object by mechanical processes and through infallible means, in which, consequently, moral action counts for nothing."

We must question this division of repetition into *inventive* repetition (imitation in the stronger sense) and *material* repetition: do mechanical processes of repetition or reproduction truly exist that can be applied directly to preexisting "objects"? Can nature be "mechanically" reproduced, and what does it mean to reproduce works? This is a question that we are about to ask Walter

Benjamin, who uses the term *reproduction* (*Reproduktion*) in a very broad sense. In fact, no means of artificially "reproducing" natural things exists, only the means of *production* that allow for a proliferation of products (for example, with the help of a mold or a matrix). In this sense, photography is not a process of "reproduction" but of producing images, first singly (the daguerreotype without a negative) and then in multiples. Its appearance posed the question of the status and the function of these hardly recognizable images.

Mechanized Reproduction

Walter Benjamin was one of the first to perceive the profound changes that new techniques like photography and cinema brought about in the domain of the arts. He contemplated in particular the effects of mass production and wide distribution of works and the consequences with regard to the value, the market, the destination of works, the public and mass consumption. Thus *The Work of Art in the Age of Mechanical Reproduction*[26] remains a major reference. In discussing a new period of art, Benjamin helps define the destiny of art in the modern epoch.

Nevertheless, by putting these questions under the jurisdiction of the idea of *reproduction*, he continues to some extent to look back to the old methods of artwork *production*. Especially with regard to photography, he is more concerned with the question of proliferation, of producing multiple prints, than with the originality of the photographic process, which he tends to neglect.

The very title of Benjamin's study poses the following problem: on the one hand, the new techniques cease to be neutralized and made into instruments; they transform art decisively enough to move it into a new *epoch*. Thus there is a modernity, an irreversibility, to the time of photography. On the other hand, these same techniques are approached mainly from the general idea of *reproduction.* Benjamin primarily examines the photography *of* works of art and not the photograph *as* art or original object, whereas in taking photographs of a painting, a cathedral, or any other "subject," we would no longer say that we were making "reproductions." Thus, the category of "reproduction" deserves to be examined.

In Benjamin's text, the division among original production, manual reproduction, and mechanized reproduction does not, *in principle*, break with the classical distinction between manual and mechanized reproduction or with Quatremère de Quincy's system of classifying imitations. Mechanized reproduction is similar to Quatremère's "material imitation," which implies only mechanical processes. But in saying that, we cannot ignore the decisive step taken by Benjamin that leads to recognizing in new "reproductive processes" like photography, the birth of autonomous artistic means and the appearance of original works themselves. Indeed, Benjamin stresses that unlike the old ones, these works are meant to be "reproduced" in great number. But to clarify: is it necessary to use this same word—*reproduction*—to speak of the proliferation of prints and to designate the photographic process itself, as Benjamin does? In doing so, isn't photography placed under the auspices of *mechanical repetition* and identical reproduction—which it is not?

Indeed, in Benjamin's well-known text, the term *reproduction* is used in a loose enough way to designate totally different operations, such as *to copy* a work manually (that is, to try to remake it), *to photograph* (especially to photograph a work), or to mechanically *multiply* copies of an initial image (graphic or photographic). These three operations cannot be included under the category of "reproductive processes for the image" without creating troublesome confusions.

But within these new "mechanized" processes, it would be useful to distinguish between the *original production techniques* for an object (for example, a photograph) and the techniques—related, it is true—for *multiplying* these objects or works. It is not because multiple prints can be made that the photograph is essentially a technique of reproduction. Moreover, the first photos, produced according to the technique of Niepce and Daguerre, were not "reproducible."

Thus Benjamin believes he can say that a work of art—painting or architecture—is "reproduced" by the photograph, designating the work photographed as the "original" (in relation to its photographic "reproduction"). Even though this use of the term is still common today, it is inexact because it erases the specificity of the photographic image. This explains how Benjamin was able to write about the photo as "mechanized reproduction": "It can reveal aspects of the *original* (*Ansichten des Originals*) not accessible to the naked eye but only to the adjustable lens." Or again: "Mechanized reproduction assures the *original* the ubiquity of which it is naturally deprived . . . it allows it to offer itself to the perception in the form of photography. . . . The cathedral leaves its site to enter an amateur's studio."

But the cathedral has not left its site. The photograph cannot be said to deprive the so-called original of its *authenticity* because a photo is not a copy or a reproduction lacking materiality (Benjamin speaks of an image "from which all materiality has withdrawn").

Because nothing has "withdrawn" from the photo—on the contrary, something very physical, the light, has come to leave its imprint, producing an absolutely novel object. If one is attentive to the originality of this process, if the specific nature of this light impression is carefully extricated, as it is today,[27] then the ambiguous use of the term *reproduction* disappears. That is not yet the case with Benjamin, who uses it at the very beginning of his text, in the sense of "copy": "It is fundamental that the work has always been reproducible. What people had done, others could always do again." Thus the possibility of *redoing what has been done* is reproduction in a basic sense, in the sense of the copy, the replica, even the fake. The copy assumes a numerical and possibly a qualitative difference between an *original* work, unique or produced "singly," and its copy, executed through the same means. Benjamin considers this copy or imitation of a work (*Nachbildung*) as a manual and artisanal mode of reproduction that is distinct from *mechanized* reproduction (*technische Reproduktion*). These two "reproductions" are thus distinguished from each other quantitatively (produced singly or mass produced) and according to their process (manual or mechanical). Nevertheless, can we speak of reproduction in these two cases? In the first, an artisan or an artist *remakes* the same work *with the same means* and the same materials—and the greatest artists are thus copied themselves, like Chardin. In the second case, an image of the thing or the work is produced *by other means* and with other materials. Thus, it would be better not to use the same category in the two cases.

Even before assessing all the effects of reproducing in great number, Benjamin also formulates a critique here of all "reproduction," artisanal or not, in the name of the uniqueness of the original and the authenticity of the work: *"The components of authenticity resist any reproduction, not only mechanized reproduction."*[28] He reminds us that the authority of the *original* has never been contested and that in comparison with its manual reproduction, it "easily exposes" the reproduction to be a "fake." Thus the problem of mechanized reproduction stems from a conception of artwork as essentially *nonreproducible.*

This authority of the "original," not to speak of this worship of authenticity, is not at all self-evident. Besides the hasty way in which Benjamin treats the question of fakes and does not treat the question of replicas, he leaves obscured the moral, legal, and economic dimensions of the idea of the copy. The value of the original comes above all from the potential for the copy to be theft. To copy is to execute—with the talent necessary for such execution—

according to the model created by another. In this sense, other things besides artworks can be copied, as counterfeiting proves.

The idea of originality, as opposed to the copy, is more that of the novelty of an invention (formal or technical) than that of uniqueness and of the here and now. The invention of a machine or the production of a prototype is no less "original" than that of an artwork. In the end, the means for copying an artwork or a "prototype" can as easily be manual as mechanical.

The valorization of the original generally responds to the need for protecting the property rights for the invention and any financial implications. Moreover, that is why instituting patents or production rights protects the author from possible copies whenever a creation lends itself to mass production. But if the use of the *photocopy* and all those pirated recordings deprive authors and producers of their commercial rights, *photography* is not primarily a means of reproduction; it is an original means of producing images.

Thus, within the arts termed *multiple*, we must distinguish between the techniques of original *production* (engraving, photography, recording . . .) and the techniques of *multiplication* (making prints) with which they are associated. Neither of the two resembles the copy. Their processes, their media, their tools, their actions, are specific. Benjamin writes hastily that with wood engraving, graphic technique "was for the first time mechanically reproducible." But wood engraving is not pencil or ink drawing; it is a whole other technique. Likewise, incising metal and inking it in metal engraving is not drawing. Moreover, it is not derived from drawing but from *niello*, a decorative technique consisting of inlaying certain metals, like gold or silver, with the help of a black substance (the niello). The idea of replacing the niello with ink made the engraving technique possible: first impressing the original plate onto paper and then allowing many "prints" to be made. Thus, engraving is not a simple technique of "reproduction" but the combination of many techniques, manual and mechanical, even if the engraver can subsequently transpose a drawing onto an engraving in order to multiply it. This technique includes the processes for producing a unique *original* (the plate) and duplication techniques.

The unfortunate ambiguity maintained by the use of the word *original* also shows up in the use of the word *image*. In the very first two pages of the text, Benjamin implements a subtle substitution. From the initial idea of reproducing *the work of art*, he shifts without warning to processes for reproducing the image: "For the first time in the reproductive processes for the image, the hand finds itself liberated." In the same passage, he compares the photographic reproduction "of the image" with the recorded reproduction of sound. But we do not photograph images. The issue here is the specific nature of photography as imprint or as "indexical" image.

This term *index* and the adjective *indexical* have been adopted from C. S. Peirce for figures obtained from an imprint. This now common usage, especially with regard to photography, is far removed from what the American semiologist called the "indexical sign." Peirce links to indexes those signs directly connected with a singular referent. Thus, the index finger pointing toward a thing is an "index," just like the word *here*, to the extent that this word is in "dynamic connection" with a singular referent. What imprints and Peirce's indexes have in common is that they both "direct the attention toward an object" because of a relationship of *contiguity* and not of resemblance.[29]

Barthes describes the indexical nature of the photograph by saying that it expresses the action of the light: "like the juice of a lemon."[30] It comes out of it, it issues from it. The fact that this imprint can—in certain cases—miraculously resemble what one sees led to the belief that the photo "reproduced" the perception and that it offered the same objects that perception did. By way of an analogy with ordinary experience, the photo fools us all and seems to offer our eyes the thing itself. That is why it appears to us as a false perception that would conceal from us the *aura* of the thing or the authenticity of the photographed work. And yet unlike the drawing, it is very much to the here and now of its "subject" that the photo refers as a trace of light on the film. The photograph can only retain this trace: its authenticity does not reside in its capacity to remake or to reproduce things; its domain is not the permanent but the luminous ephemeral phenomena. With the trace of a passing light, it retains the look—itself fleeting—of things and nothing more. Its magic is to give form and duration to these ephemera, to give a permanent and reproducible image to a fleeting appearance never to be repeated.

In this sense, the photographic image is not so far from the image that Baudelaire asks the modern artist to reconstruct. But instead of seizing the momentary impression produced by things *on the mind*, it is the luminous impression of things *on the film*, without the mediation of the imagination or of subjective interiority. It is not, of course, that the photographer does nothing; on the contrary, he participates fully in the creation of the image through all kinds of choices and actions (subject, centering, light, zoom, and so forth), but he does not imagine, he "images," and beyond all his strategies, the photo will, in the end, have the objectivity of a material trace.

And, just as Roland Barthes writes, it is very much as a material trace, an indisputable objective index of something that, at one precise moment, has been seized by a camera and can now again be seized by our gaze, that the photo has poignancy.[31] Again, it is because it was "mechanical" that the trace remains the anonymous testimony of what was, showing, like the shot of the park in *Blow Up* or a photo taken from a satellite, that something was there—revealed afterward by an imprint—that perhaps no one had seen. In stopping time, in fixing the imprint of things in a motionless image that the gaze can now explore, any photo offers, forever, the *never seen*. And it offers the *never imagined*, since if it is considered a faculty of the mind, the imagination cannot draw from itself what the imprint of one luminous body on another offers.

In this sense, the photographic image was *unimaginable*. It was very much an event and opened a new epoch. By *unimaginable*, we mean here that it is unable to be anticipated by an autonomous imagination that claims not to be dependent, for its own inventions, on technical inventions. Photography cannot enter into a history of art over which this interior and entirely spiritual imagination rules. Rather than renew the old war between art and techniques or think about new techniques beginning from the old ones, isn't it necessary to rethink art beginning from technical invention, including the invention of instruments, processes, apparatuses, and actions? Not only do more or less mechanized epochs of "art" exist, but—sticking very close to what is most novel in Benjamin—we ought to say that all *the arts* are always inscribed, and sometimes invented, within a moment in the history of techniques.

THE EPOCH OF PHANTOMS

. . . . .

PARADOXICALLY, our epoch, which must learn to free itself from the past, is also the time of recording techniques. The thinking about passage and passing is contemporary with the development of techniques for conserving the traces of people and things, their visible appearance or audible expression. Is this a contradiction? It does not seem to be. Conserving the traces aids in remembering and forgetting at the same time. The material trace serves to support the subjective recollection of old experiences, but the memory is also freed from its responsibilities by *externalizing* itself in the support materials (writing, pictures, computer data).

In constituting a material memory of movements, along with cinema, the techniques for conserving and reproducing traces also allow us to have at our disposal *passage* itself and no longer just the more or less fixed representation of movement. Elusive as they were in the past, all fragments of time (of movement) seemed transient, and only supposedly lasting things could lay claim to some actual reality. Representing the fleeting was difficult, indeed even prohibited by the classical aesthetic. By granting movement the possibility of being "reproduced," recordings conferred on it a new status. But that does not mean that the trace is a good thing for the memory.

It can no longer be said, as in the past, that words vanish. Now they can remain just as easily as writing can, and the tone of a voice or a simple sigh can be imprinted and heard again. Anything that is recordable, sounds or images, can claim to *pass* again, multiple times, to be heard or seen once more. Still, it is necessary for someone to hear or look at the recording, which, in fact, happens quite rarely.

Indeed, a considerable gap exists between the mass of private and public recordings and the use to which they are put, as if the functions of conservation or archival storage—indeed even the act of recording itself—were more important than the use of the archives for recollection, information, or history. Even amateur photography indicates that the moments of taking the pictures are more important than the—finally very rare—moments of looking at the snapshots. At best, after a quick glance, the photos accumulate in boxes. Taking the shot—whatever the results—can be analyzed as a significant action, a way of giving meaning to a lived experience even before the moment of the development of the image around which discourse will be possible.[1] The photos that make it into the family album are used especially in the integration ritual according to which they are piously revealed to a new family member, these images of a history that then becomes something of one's own.[2]

But we must not confuse the effects of cinema and those of photography on our experience of time. The first revolution involved the indexical image, imprint or trace, with its magic effect; the second involved the "moving picture" or "*l'image mouve-mentée*" (as they said at the very beginning of cinema).

Photography, which is our particular concern, is divided—for the photographer—into distinct moments: the time of the shot, the time of the development, and the time of looking at the image. Each of these moments has its duration, and to a certain extent, each action has its autonomy—but we cannot understand the *effect* of the image without considering photography's particular temporality, that is, the temporal gap with itself. Taking the photo occurs in the time of expectation, pending the viewing of the print (we still do not know what it is going to reveal), while the developed image gives a retrospective view (thus, *that was*). The effects of photography cannot be understood without this essential delaying of the view. The photograph presents something different from its object, locating the one who takes it between the *not yet* and the *already no more* of the visible—thus producing the anachronism.

The desire to record, even if it is not later "developed" (in both senses of the word), includes the possibility of a return: the trace will be able to come back—and this very possibility programs both the forgetting (since we know that the trace guarantees a material memory) and the remembering (I will be able to have access to it again). In counting on a retrospective vision, in entrusting my memory to the material trace, I can save myself the effort of a subjective recollection, indeed even of an attentive look at the present. That is how the amateur photographer risks depriving himself of any present. In fact, it is risky to sacrifice present experience or subjective memory to recordings because—apart from being different in nature—the material memory is much less sure than we would like to believe it to be. First of all, this is because the techniques do not rule out accident (equipment failure, bad recording conditions, and the like) and, second, because the progress of the techniques themselves, with the appearance of new processes and equipment, renders older recordings useless quite quickly. Already we can no longer easily view amateur films shot twenty years ago or listen to 78- or even 45- or 33-rpm records. Old recordings must continually be saved by transferring them to a different medium; otherwise they will remain forever secret and inaccessible memories. Here we can see the advantage of the book on paper which, as long as it can be conserved, needs only a concentrated gaze to be read once more.

Of course, it is never the reality itself that is recorded, as the deceptive term *reproduction* might suggest.[3] Certain physical phenomena can leave a trace on a medium that then produces impressions similar to those made on us by the things themselves (provided that these traces offer a definite analogy to certain sensations, as in the case of photographs). Thus the recording detaches certain qualities from the perceptible reality. It is never the things themselves that can be conserved but only this or that quality of theirs, like a sort of skin, a sort of film of the real.

With the trace of light, a past event leaves a visible aspect of itself—like those stars that we still can see, even though they no longer exist. The image of the thing is propagated in time and space thanks to the voyage of light (photography is a method of propagation by light). A passing "phenomenon" that continues to appear to us when it has disappeared thus acquires, through its trace, a new form of "presence" having nothing in common with a painted or drawn image. Whereas a drawing is the trace of an action and constitutes a figure constructed by someone, a trace of the light is left in an almost autonomous fashion. Perceived later, this trace creates the illusion of contemporaneity between the thing photographed and the one who observes it, thereby confusing their respective times. The specter of the thing appears to the observer like a ghost from another time, whereas by contemplating the image, the observer himself goes off to haunt another time.

A transformation in perception took place with the possibility of having available material traces of movement, of analyzing them, of making variations in them. Whereas the close-up expands space under our eyes, slow motion expands time and functions, according to Benjamin, as a magnifying glass for time (*eine*

Zeitlupe) allowing for an absolutely novel experience of movement. Like photography, cinema is not a new means of "representing" a visible and already seen world but an unprecedented observation technique. The possibility of observing movement beginning with images in motion, of slowing it down or speeding it up, offers novel means of representing time and produces new models for thought.

From the inception of chronophotography[4] up to the cinema and digitalization techniques, the "moving" image thus took the place of immobile figures as the *model* of representation and intelligibility.

Perhaps philosophy was never independent of techniques of representation, even if it was unaware of this dependence. Mental representations, long considered the result of "interior" operations, could well have been conditioned by so-called exterior material representations. Thus for a time, the concept and the image shared the claim of offering permanence to being.

The Image and Suspended Time

Reading Plato, we must remember that the Greek word *idéa* evokes the permanent aspect of a thing. Thus, when the philosopher defines reality beginning from ideas (*idéa*), he has in mind that which does not vary in it. The "idea" is the intellectual grasping of an eternal reality. It no doubt satisfies a desire for continuity and stability. But the privileged position of this immutability also sheds much needed light when considering the relationship between the thinking and the material methods of representation in an epoch. Thus, the Greek meaning of *idéa*—and so the privilege given to the permanent aspect of a thing—corresponds to the abstract and lasting aspect of drawn images or sculptured works. Of course, we know that Plato opposed the intelligibility of the idea to the visibility of the image. It remains true nonetheless that as immutable models or paradigms, ideas have those abstract and atemporal characteristics that make them similar to diagrams, in other words, to drawings.

Metaphysics has always wanted to base the image on the idea without examining closely enough what the idea could owe to the image. Nevertheless, couldn't those operations attributed to the mind, for example, memory, be understood as internalizations of technical operations? By reversing the hierarchy established by Italian theorists from the "mannerist" period,[5] according to which the "external" drawing is the expression of a preliminary "internal" drawing (the *disegno interno*), we may wonder whether the interior drawing is not already the mental mark of a graphic or schematic operation—that is, a technical operation.

It is often said that memory, incapable of retaining an infinite number of aspects, schematizes, simplifies, sacrifices shapes and details, to keep only a broad, abstract mental picture. Thus Baudelaire places memory at the origin of drawing and attributes to it the power to synthesize.[6] But if we can admit that drawing is done "from memory"—since the artist retains from the model only its general aspect and forgets the details—we could also say that memory imitates drawing, that memory itself schematizes. In proceeding by abstraction, it operates like drawing.

After all, from what does the drawing abstract? First of all, from *time*, that is, from movement. Classical theory asks the painter to suspend time—whether art is supposed to present the essence of things, their eternal nature, or whether it is supposed to avoid the pitfall that, for it, would be representing the passing.

Lessing, for example, explicitly condemns the representation of the transitory and fleeting.[7] Indeed, the work imposes a duration on the representation; it must not show what, naturally, does not last. If an ephemeral phenomenon, like a cry or a laugh, were represented, it would offer the viewer an aspect that went against nature. For Lessing, a pictorial image of passing crises would be as intolerable as one of Medea killing her children or Ajax in a rage. Thus the artist must show Medea *before* her crime, as Timonaque did, or Ajax *after* his fury and leave to the viewer the freedom of imagining, rather than seeing, those extreme moments. In preferring the moment of reflection (the moment of planning or of remorse) to the moment of action for his figures, the painter suspends movement and thus time, which is appropriate to his art.

Louis Marin analyzes the perplexities of representing movement in classical painting, saying that a "deposition of time"[8] is made, in the sense that deposition can also mean *to commit to the grave*. It is not so much "the moment" that the painter cannot show—because the moment is always constructed, it is the immobilization and negation of time—it is the temporality of a movement or passage. The examples Louis Marin gives illustrate the difficulties of representing time pictorially—in this case, the time necessary for cutting off a head and killing someone. Here then are three scenes of sacrifice: the *Martyrdom of Saint Blaise*, a Romanesque fresco in the Berzé-la-Ville chapel, and two Caravaggio paintings, *Judith and Holopherne* and *The Sacrifice of Isaac*. In each of these examples, the representation shows an action that cannot take place in the painting, the scene of a death that does not come to *pass*. In the *Martyrdom of Saint Blaise*, the fresco shows the before and after of a decapitation itself unrepresentable (the sword raised by the henchman about to strike and, beside it, the already cut head as it rolls and falls). In *Judith and Holopherne*, Judith's sword is very much "in the process" of cutting Holopherne's neck, but precisely the way this sword is stopped in the middle of the neck shows that the painting will never finish sacrificing Holopherne. Finally, Abraham is painted with knife raised over his son who is screaming in terror while his arm is seized by the angel who stops the action. According to Marin, the viewer discerns the suspension of his own execution here, the reprieve of his own death. I should add that as soon as Abraham's arm is immobilized by the painting and the murder is definitively suspended, the painting inevitably erases everything that makes Abraham's trial horrifying, that is, all the time during which he prepares himself for the sacrifice of his son. No image can make real that terrible time of what Kierkegaard called the "infinite resignation of Abraham."[9] By simultaneously presenting us with the imminent death of Isaac and the emissary who is going to save him, the painting shows that the sacrifice will not take place and spares us the time of Abraham's trial—and Isaac's—that is, the terrible time of the decree of death.

That time, the time of waiting, of coming death, of death that is going to come, the cinema has made into one of its principal domains. The effect of *suspense* belongs to the arts capable of stalling—or of hastening—their movements: literature, film, music.

Let us return to the relationship between thought and drawing. For metaphysics, at least until Kant, thinking could not be compared or likened to a technical operation. In principle, the object thought of or represented *mentally* precedes any spatial representation, any drawn figure. As conceived through an idealist perspective, mental representation is not dependent on available material images.

This conception allows for leaving the intelligible and the perceptible, the concept and the image, within the exteriority of an encounter, for subordinating the artistic representation to intellectual concepts and for ignoring the empirical genesis of forms or concepts.

The difficulty for this dualistic thinking is reuniting what it began to separate—the intelligible and the perceptible, the concept and the image, the understanding and the sensibility, the transcendental and the empirical. If the concept is independent of the image, the problem is knowing how to apply one to the other. Kant resolved this problem by inventing the *schemata*, the art of constructing *schemas*, which are intermediary figures between empirical intuitions (particular) and concepts (general).

The Schema of a Quadruped

For Kant, if schematism is primarily the application of pure concepts of understanding (that is, the categories),[10] it also plays a role in defining empirical concepts like the concept of a dog. This concept relates immediately to a schema, that is, to a rule "by which my *imagination* expresses in general the *figure of a quadruped* without being applied to something in particular."[11]

The concept of dog is not pure, but neither is it reducible to the perception of this or that particular dog (Fido or Snoopy). Immediately this is a *figure*, schema or image-schema, neither general nor particular. In other words, it is simultaneously a general image and a perceptible concept, a kind of type or "monogram" that functions as a rule in such a way as to determine how a thing must appear in order to conform to this or that concept (or again, how the image of a thing must be presented to respond to the concept of that thing). Thus I must have at my disposal the schema of a quadruped in order to judge whether or not the animal that I am now seeing is really a dog.

Heidegger comments at length on this status of schema by defining it as a sort of drawing (*Auszeichnen*).[12] Indeed, Kant describes the schematizing operation as a rule of "construction," thus classifying it as a mental activity—but also as a technical process. Insofar as it is constructed, the image-schema introduces into the imagination a share of representation. To recognize a dog assumes the ability *to draw* it mentally. What mental faculty could *imagine* schemas if it did not rely on the power of *imaging*, on the actual production of certain forms or structures that really do retain only the most general and most commonly shared traces of things? The possibility of drawing some dog or another (mentally or manually), that is, of producing a schema: isn't this of the same order as the operation consisting of thinking about the concept of dog? For an empirical concept of this type, there is no fundamental difference between the concept and the schema.

Thus, Kantian schematization is supposed to provide an intermediary between the general concept of a thing and an image, always particular. But we could also consider the schema as deconstructing the opposition between the two and show that it is only a special image, that is, a *schema* in the ordinary sense of the word, meaning diagram or sketch. But neither Kant nor Heidegger classes the schema with the category of drawings, because it would be linked dangerously close to the image and call into question the distinction between concept and image. Conversely, maintaining the clear opposition between the two plays a role in Heidegger's reading of Kant, all the more easily because Heidegger uses the word *image* (*Bild*) in the simple sense of "view" or reproduction: the image is what a being offers of itself to sight or even the copy or the reproduction of the thing. For example, a death mask and a photograph are images and very distinctive examples, since it is a matter here of traces, imprints. Thus, there is nothing surprising about the image being defined here as *repraesentatio singularis*, and the philosopher saying about the concept (general) that it cannot be *put into image*.[13] But considered in its broader sense and its constructed reality as a drawing, a plan, a schema, the image not only is capable of providing the aspect of one particular thing, but it also offers a "general" aspect; it can be valid "for several," can remain true despite the changes in things over time, and thus can closely approach the concept.

Mental representations therefore can be associated with material techniques of representation, indeed, even seem to be dependent on the forms that those techniques produce. Certain ways of seeing or thinking are contemporaneous with drawing (still today, of course), while others are contemporaneous with photography and cinema. Thinking is structured according to plastic forms as much as through discursive forms. Our mental representations are nurtured on images and things seen, just as our internal monologues silently imitate discourse. This considerably reduces the field of what is called *interiority*—if such a thing exists.

Thus we can no longer ask the old question of the relationship between concept and image without inscribing it within the problem of the relationship between thinking and its forms in general, that is, the *figures* that it constructs and on which it operates, whether those of language or of visual forms. An "idea" in the sense of the mental grasping of something cannot be isolated from that part of representation that it implies. Paul Valéry, the great forerunner in this area, understood the importance of figures for a kind of modern thinking freed from dualism, especially for scientific thought. Graphics, curves, and diagrams create a form of thought and knowledge for which the distinction between the eye and the mind no longer makes sense. Thus:

> The great invention of rendering the laws *perceptible to the eye* and *readable on sight* is incorporated into knowledge and in some way doubles the world of experience with a visible world of curves, surfaces, diagrams, that transposes properties into figures according to which by following the inflections with the eye, we experience, through consciousness of that movement, the feeling of the vicissitudes of greatness.[14]

Among the "traces of the things themselves," as Valéry says, there are not only diagrams, there are also *photograms*. Photography and cinema produce images that are incorporated into our thinking. The indexical image not only wreaks havoc with our visual experience and our means of knowing, but it also transforms our memory.

The Scent of a Woman

It is often believed that images "recall the past" and make the living memory of a lived moment or a loved person come back. But conversely, the photo can screen the memory. Proust accurately evokes the disappointment felt looking at "the photographs of someone and recalling him less well than by being content with thinking about him."[15]

The image really is different in nature from the lived experience, even the visual experience, and cannot restore it. The memory of someone is the vague impression of a presence, an attitude, an "air"; it is the memory of a style, not of an image. It is the memory of the impression that the other made on me—something undefinable: a relationship between us, the memory of shared pleasure or complicity. Nothing objective. There is this sense of secret traces about it, traces of emotion, independent of any visible image. Thus, the memory owes practically nothing to the image.

Of course, the resemblance between the photographic image and the visible can also serve as an aid to memory. But from the point of view of memory, the value of a photo is not that. To the value of image, linked to the resemblance, the photo adds a value of imprint. These two values, or functions, are not identical, since an image is not necessarily a trace of the thing it imitates and since, inversely, the value of a trace does not stem solely from resemblance. The scent of a woman is a trace; it retains something of her presence without in any way resembling her. And even the trace of her lipstick on a handkerchief, her foot on the ground, or her body on a cushion are not images but the persistent effects of her presence. The trace, or imprint, is in a relationship of physical contiguity with a thing or person, and that is why it becomes the object of a particular pathos and *worship*. The imprint touches us because it has been touched itself and because it speaks to us of presence and absence at the same time—"as much the contact of loss as the loss of contact."[16]

Only the indexical image is simultaneously a trace and an image and allows the worship of the imprint to be united with the pleasure of the image. Outside any artistic or utilitarian concern, taking a picture is first of all wanting to retain the *imprint* of someone or something, even before wanting to make an *image* of it. From the time the young Dibutades invented drawing by tracing the contour of the *shadow* of her beloved, to keep the imprint of a face has been to touch it. The idea that drawing first followed the trace of a beloved face (its shadow) is a lovely myth because it unites the caress, the imprint, and the image. Nothing proves that it is only a matter of seeing in that "circumscription of the shadow" (*circumductio umbrae*)[17] or that the gaze does not *touch* what it gazes at. (Let us leave to the Puritan philosophers the naïve belief that the eye is distant and respectful.)

Thus the trace assumes the role of corporeal relic for the thing: with it, an absent body is still there as a vestige, from which we get the religious or private worship of *relics*. When the imprint forms a resembling image at the same time, as with the Shroud of Turin, supposedly retaining the trace of Christ's face, we are dealing with "a photo of a particular kind."[18] The union of the imprint value and the image value gives photography its magic power and its particular aura. And if through resemblance, it is the appearance itself that survives in the photographic or cinematic trace, then the images become veritable *phantoms*, and it is not surprising that they have been seen as such since their inception.

Does our own use of photography escape this "animism"? Nothing could be less certain. It is not that we are naïve but that we have become capable of creating *real phantoms*. Like Gilles Deleuze, recording televised interviews with Claire Parnet to be broadcast "after his death,"[19] we can now program our afterlife as a ghost. Besides, the phantom is a figure of the materialist imagination—because those who believe in pure spirits cannot believe in ghosts and do not have any need for them. Phantoms are the vestiges, the remains, the corporeal traces.

Whereas the photographic image reduced the role of verbal description, the cinematic account, documentary or fiction, deprived discourse of its monopoly on narrative. Our universe is peopled with faces of the dead as well as the living, to the point that we might wonder whether our descendants will not one day be tempted by a new iconoclasm to escape the armies of phantoms that we will have left them.

A Mixed Memory

The importance of phantoms is that they constitute a kind of savings for the memory. If it is possible to retain the past in such a way that it can return or *pass again*—like a televised interview—if it is possible to materially and objectively conserve the memory of someone's words and expression, to the least trembling of the voice, the blinking of an eye, then thought can be spared the effort of an *internal* conservation, in other words, a recollection, belonging to the subjective memory. The *Abécédaire* does not replace Deleuze's books; it is something entirely different. It leaves an astonishing trace of the philosopher's art of speaking, with his gestures, his stresses, his way of drawing out the beginning of a searched-for phrase, his slightly haughty smile, his aristocratic and deceptively familiar style, and the immense pleasure he takes in bringing concepts to life.

The image as vestige thus competes with recollection: it serves the memory less than it supplants it. It already replaces it because it is there, perceptible, real, present, whereas a memory is vague and elusive. It replaces it again when the memory of the image (and no longer the image itself) masks the memory of the thing and screens any return to the past. It is then incorporated into the whole of subjective memory, like any other recollection. This incorporation finally does not permit natural memory to be opposed to artificial memory, living internal memory to an exterior memory, confined to traces.

To take photographs is to produce a material memory capable of making up for the frailty of ordinary memory. Plato would not have failed to conclude that photography, like writing, seriously threatens memory (in the sense of a faculty of the soul). But it threatens only a naturally faltering, essentially amnesiac memory. Like all other processes of recording, drawing, or writing, it helps constitute a *mixed memory*, in which the lived merges with the traces. Thus "natural" memory incorporates artificial images that function as the equivalents of lived experience. The ghosts live among us, just as in *The Purple Rose of Cairo*[20] the actors leave the screen and mix with the life of the viewers.

ANACHRONISMS OF ART: STYLE AND MEDIUM

. . . . .

THERE IS NOTHING obvious about using the term *anachronism* to refer to works of art. This term is more often applied to the world of technical objects: thus it would seem anachronistic today to cook over a wood fire, to grind coffee by hand, or to travel by horse. The use of the term here implies improvements that are sometimes accompanied by inconveniences but that exclude any return to the past. The use of outdated objects is thus "tainted"[1] with anachronism.

There is no evidence—very much to the contrary, in fact—that such irreversibility exists in the history of art. And nevertheless, there too, the impression of anachronism exists. As we shall see, it does not necessarily have to be understood in a pejorative sense, even if it generally expresses depreciation of a work betraying its own time and thus running counter to modernity.

Thus, for Pierre Francastel,[2] an art historian and sociologist, all work is inscribed within the context of a specific culture, and artistic forms belong to the "general movement" of the civilization that is their own. Artistic currents that claim to perpetuate immutable forms are in fact attached to old models, conceived in a different context, in other words, to more or less anachronistic forms. Thus, in certain cases, the illusion of an eternal art might support outmoded ("*dépassé*") art forms. "Living" works are those that find their source in their own epoch, whereas "dead" works perpetuate old forms. The idea of context refers here to the intellectual and technical conditions—that is, social—that gave rise to the works and that make them respond more or less to their own epoch. Certain technical innovations seem to require new forms, for example, in architecture, whereas the traditional models inhibit or betray the possibilities of innovation. Later I will reconsider this kind of time lag.

Thus denouncing the anachronism is usually part of a historicist view of art, and if Francastel refrains from any progressivism,[3] he valorizes modernity through the irreversibility of movement and the emphasis placed on the new. The rejection of the anachronism is more radical still from a teleological perspective. Attachment to the past or returning to old forms thus appears suspect, indeed even regressive, in light of the necessary movement of history.

The notion of progress valorizes the new but cannot manage without permanence. Progress is not conceivable without some authority that progresses and thus remains the same through its transformations. It assumes a subject or a substance that does not die, that does not disappear with time—that accumulates knowledge, for example, or perfects an action. With Hegel, it is Spirit that denies itself and does away with itself in conserving itself, according to a dialectical movement that condemns repetition. In reconciling life and death (the living reappropriating the dead, the dead letting themselves be "born again" in the living), the history of Spirit means that the past neither dies nor returns, since it is "conserved" in the present. The subject of that history itself does not pass and thus cannot return; the logic of the phoenix condemns the anachronism and rules out phantoms.

But the anachronism is precisely not the permanent: it is not what survives or lives on; it is what reappears in some way shifted forward or backward in time. This displacement can also occur in the other direction, when the recent is projected into the past. That is why attributing behavior or thinking belonging to the present to ancient societies is classically condemned as anachronistic.

In Praise of the Anachronism

We owe to Nicole Loraux a just plea "for a controlled exercise in anachronism"[4] in history. Far from rejecting the principle of epochs' or cultures' alterity in the name of classical humanism and an eternal human essence, the historian stresses that alongside historic temporality with its share of irreversibility are those passions or situations that repeat themselves, that come back. Among the recurring motifs that especially interest Nicole Loraux, for example, is political amnesty. What does it mean, she wonders, for a democratic city-state to pledge "not to recall the misfortunes of the past"? Can the Athens of 403 B.C. shed light on something of our own problems with the past? Underneath "time vectorized by history" the historian encounters another time, a time in which instead of passing, certain events or certain passions return.

The question of a repetition that would resist the progress of vectorial or dialectical history also arises in the history of art. Today, Georges Didi-Huberman considers the anachronism to call into question the conception of art history that depends on categories of early, mature, and declining—like Vasari's conception.[5] He refers especially to the wax portrait that had struck Schlosser[6] for its lack of evolution, as if this archaic object had returned, traversing the ages, resistant to any "sense of history." A good example of survival, or of "coming back from the dead," is given by

Georges Didi-Huberman in *Phasmes*:[7] it is a matter of a terra-cotta piece, discovered by chance at the *mercato di figurine* on Rome's Navona Piazza, in which he recognizes a deeply buried Etruscan figure. This find leads the Roman stroller to question not only the survival of forms through time but also their displacement from one category of objects to another (toys, sacred objects, works of art . . .).

The importance to survival in the history of art here echoes the works of Aby Warburg[8] and, even more distantly, those of the ethnologist E. B. Tylor, who considered beliefs and customs to be the preservation of ancient laws in a transformed world.[9]

In a letter to Fliess, Freud refers to the same model (the survival of ancient laws, *fueros*, in certain regions of Spain) to describe the psychoanalytical concept of *fixation*, that is, a subject's tendency to repeat old modes of satisfaction, whatever the circumstances. Freud considers fixation an anachronism in the libidinal history and compares it to a holdover: "Thus we find ourselves in the presence of an anachronism: in a certain province, *fueros* still exist, traces of the past have survived."[10] I will return to the idea of fixation later, which could very well also have meaning in the history of images and forms in general.

Thus, more than something permanent, the anachronism is a relic, a paradoxical holdover, displaced, chronologically strange. It always has something to do with the ghost or phantom. All the phantom's ambiguity, like our ambivalent relationship to it, comes from the way it is a return of the past as past or the dead as dead. Unlike the idea of simple conservation, it presupposes finitude and death, which it then transgresses.

Classical thought cannot consider the anachronism because it does not really believe in death (either what dies is nothing, or it becomes something else historically and thus does not die). Rather, the relic is the figure of a return that evades or fools disappearance—without denying it. To survive is a way of going against death here below and not of continuing to be, in this world or in another, or even of dialectically preserving the dead in a new life.

What works of art, what objects, are capable of such transgressions? We just mentioned the example of wax portraits, but isn't the portrait in general, by its very principle, an anachronistic image? Isn't imitation itself a factor of repetition shifted in time and thus of anachronism?

Painting, which can "render present those who are absent,"[11] as Alberti claimed, is capable of producing the frightening effect of a ghost: "Plutarch recounts that Cassander, one of Alexander's generals, began to tremble all over seeing an image of the deceased and recognizing in it the majesty of the king."[12] If Cassander is troubled by an image in this way, it is not that the image creates an effective illusion of the dead emperor's presence; it is that as a ghost, it renders present the one who, at the same time, remains absent, who is therefore neither past nor present. It is this in-between, between life and death, between presence and absence, that makes the portrait of the deceased an anachronism.

If modernity today consists of believing in death—as our ancestors believed in eternity or in history—it could very well require a new view of the relic, a valorization of imitation, of reproduction or repetition, as the only possibilities for enduring or for returning.

How can we explain certain rituals or holidays—and no doubt we should say all rituals—without taking into account the power of repetition or the pleasure of repetition for its own sake? The idea of an afterlife (*Nachleben* in German) allows Aby Warburg to describe in the history of works or of cultures, repetitions, returns, echoes that escape the progressive, rationalist schema of history.[13] For example, he compares certain Mexican rituals with elements belonging to sixteenth-century Florentine culture. The Antelope dance, still practiced in 1895 by the Indians at Ildefonso near Santa Fe, quite a long time after the antelope herds had disappeared, seemed to him the survival of an ancient ritual.[14] Whether it is a matter of the overabundance of wax portraits in Florence's churches in the fifteenth century or the bronze portraits in the church of the Innsbruck court, Warburg suspects that these votive images are a "survival of pagan portrait art in Christian churches."[15] The historian himself does not in any way look backward toward a humanist conception that would hold history as negligible from the perspective of humanity's eternal characteristics; rather, he suggests—and in this, his view is related to Nicole Loraux's—the need to take into account a multiplicity of movements and temporalities. Thus history would involve, on the one hand, an irreversible, vectorial time in which things are transformed, indeed even progress; and, on the other hand, a time of repetition, of return, in which very obstinate things come back. Beneath the progressive time of the Enlightenment, there would have been a time for cyclical phenomena explaining the cultural and artistic correspondences between the past and the present.[16] Thus Warburg's works are inscribed in a postdialectical conception of history for which the logic of the present "overtaking" the past, the modern "passing" the ancient, coexists with certain persistent repetitions. With this double logic or double temporality, the present does not always supplant the past, and the modern does not simply take over for the ancient—according to the Hegelian or Hugolian fatalism of "this will kill that."[17]

What is more, not all repetition is necessarily deathly or indicative of inertia, as a progressive historical perspective tries to make us believe. It can also signify the resistance of beings and forms to their own disappearance. After all, life itself persists through repetition (sleeping, eating, sexual activity . . .). Procreation has an essential relationship to survival—whether parents experience the possibility of surviving through their children or whether new generations have the feeling of surviving those of their parents and ancestors. Life seems to imitate itself through the generations much more than it destroys or maintains itself. We have always known that: nature loves to repeat itself, but it also has a history, and particularly among humans the most inventive part of its conduct tends to contradict repetition. Beyond radical historicism, modernity now signifies taking into account these two movements, deconstructing the clear opposition between nature and history, the anthropological and the historical.

What is troubling about repetition is its nonrational—if not irrational—nature. Thus, the "primitive" survives in modern cultures, and magic can be contemporary with logic. Contrary to what more classical interpretations have led us to believe, the Dionysian does not succumb to the progress of the Apollonian, and pagan culture does not yield completely to Christian faith. Neither the moderns nor the ancients substituted a rational, transparent world for one animated by obscure powers. Warburg recalls that in Italy in about 520, "Antiquity was worshiped in some way in the form of a double-faced Hermes, one face dark and demonic, requiring a superstitious cult, and the other bright and Olympian, demanding aesthetic adoration."[18] Perhaps each epoch presents a double face as well.

To come back to works of art, we could say that the work would be individual caprice only if certain artistic "formulas" were not repeated and did not form what Gombrich calls a "vocabulary of art."[19] Beyond the resources of their present experience and their conscious intentions, artists take up again through style, indeed even through stereotypes, artistic formulas inherited from the past—exactly the way, in speaking, we adopt very old expressions in everyday speech.

Thus anachronism is more a rule than an exception. It expresses the recurrence of forms in different times or, again, the coexistence, within a single system, of historically heterogeneous forms or styles, in other words, to use an old word, *anachrones*.

Every world, every present, is composed of objects coming from periods or strata of different times. To take into account this "anachrony" or these anachronisms is to deny the alternative between cyclical or repetitive history, perhaps the expression of more "primitive" forces, and linear history, progressive, irreversible, and cumulative.

We cannot imagine time as either a circle or a line but, rather, as an infinite spiraling curl. This figure corresponds quite well to the idea of time that the generational difference gives us, that is, the idea of histories that overlap. If one dealt only with the time of one's own life or if our species could have—an absurd fiction—been born and died all at once, that is, in one single time, time would have no depths for us. It is strange that the generational difference has been so routinely ignored by philosophy. Reason is located within the atemporal, or else it hypothesizes a homogeneous temporality. Nevertheless, it is through others that time opens out infinitely beyond our present life; it is through ascendants and descendants that the past and the future are conceivable as opposing directions in a history where I was not and where I will no longer be. The idea of another time does not refer to the continuity of an abstract chronology but to the *time of another*, as the past evokes the history of others. Can we seal up this discontinuity of generations by merging them into a single history, or must we accept the heterogeneity of histories that are interwoven together and overlap one another without ever coming to an end or being concealed? The experience of time is one of a heterogeneity that goes through the test of generation, that is, through the perpetual time lag of births and deaths. This difference forms the basis of our right to succeed our ascendants and to survive those who have had their time. It exempts us from assuming their past as if it were our own.

Beyond the arts, objects, and rituals, the idea of survival is further applied by Warburg to the historian himself, whose mission it is to make the people of the past revive or survive by assembling various documents, in particular, texts and images. As time differentiates generations (or rather, generations differentiate time), death brings about a fragmentation of the remains (portraits and images on the one hand, discourse on the other). Like a filmmaker, the historian must then mount and mix anew the separate traces to once more find the voice of the dead: "The historian's devotion can restore the tone (*Klangfarbe*), the "resonant color" of these inaudible voices, if he does not retreat before the effort of reforming the natural link between speech and image."[20] Thus in one sense, the historian creates anachronistic work himself, since he contributes to the survival of works, indeed even of individuals, out of their time. In another sense, he "reestablishes the synchrony of images and discourse,"[21] as Philippe-Alain Michaud says, and in that way, he combats the diachronic dispersion of traces. Thus it would fall to history to repair, redo, or reweave what time undoes, to make time *pass again* in a text. The historian Warburg is a *passer of time*, in the sense that the writer Benjamin was. But if the historian can work toward making the past survive only by assembling traces, is it because he knows no other way of imagining that past himself and of recognizing himself in it? Again like Benjamin, Warburg lets himself be traversed by time and inhabited by the traces of a past that is not his own. He intermingles lived experience with lettered or learned experience and with the experience of images. He puts the mixed and the mixing to work. He "remounts" time.

The history in question here does not assume the permanence of an unchanged humanity. Rather, it obliges us not to want to domesticate the past too much and to accept "traveling in the depths of extinct social species."[22] It is from the depths of definitive extinctions that relics arise—strange and fascinating phantoms or remains that painfully encumber the present.

Far from valorizing the anachronism, a certain kind of modernism has wanted to extract works of art from all context and establish them in an abstract and ahistoric place. When art is defined, for example, by its removal from any use and any function, it is open to an "aesthetic" judgment, supposedly universal and disinterested, in the neutral space of the museum—real or imaginary. Of course, the statue of a god enters the "world of art" when we have stopped kneeling before it: for all that, does it exist *out of time*, and are its beauty and interest unrelated to the world from which it was born? The more familiar we are with its worship, the more successfully the statue *survives* it. And it survives differently on the street corner, where it constitutes a moving anachronism, than it does in a museum that would have it removed from the past as well as the present. When it claims to transcend time and place things in abstract non-places, the museum deprives us of the vertigo of the anachronism. Better to have the contrast between epochs, and in the expositions as well, than "the enigmatic deliverance from time" called for by Malraux for his "imaginary museum."[23] Let us prefer the collectors who—like birds, children, and old people—accumulate assorted objects to museology, if it claims to assemble works within the unity of a historic order or an absolute metaphysical foundation.

However, the anachronistic part of modernity must not allow us to neglect the role of the new and the irreversible, to which the question of techniques leads us back once again.

I have already made this point:[24] in Baudelaire's time and for many of his contemporaries, technical modernity remained foreign to artistic modernity. This conflict expressed a conception of art indifferent to the material means of executing works, supposedly entirely subject to the mind.

The attention given to production, that is, to the materiality of the work, implies, on the contrary, taking into account the technical context in which it develops and may allow for overcoming the opposition between art and technique. That is what Pierre

Francastel wanted to do by relying on the painter Delaunay's expression: "As the means, so the art."

Medium, Forms, and Materials

Francastel's interest in techniques was not unrelated to his reading of Walter Benjamin's article published in 1936: "The Work of Art in the Age of Mechanical Reproduction."[25] He cited it in *Painting and Society* in 1950,[26] stressing the importance of the newly accepted idea of medium "that shatters the classical conception or more accurately the romantic conception of the illusion." The question of the relationship between an art's possibilities and its medium had become particularly urgent, as much in architecture as with the appearance of new techniques for the image (photography and cinema).

However, if he proves attentive to the question of the medium in architecture, Francastel is less so when it is a matter of images. "Investigations into photography and film are indispensable elements in all serious study of contemporary art,"[27] he writes, nevertheless not including photographic images in contemporary art. According to him, there is "an exchange of tendencies between *the images of art* and *those of the camera*"[28]—a phrasing that clearly proves that he does not mix the two. Even if he stresses the role of centering, "mechanical" recording remains for him foreign to art in the strict sense, that is, to the creation of a language and a style.

In architecture, the appearance of new materials, like concrete at the end of the nineteenth century, or new possibilities for using iron, were not enough by themselves to change the old programs. In building the Sainte-Geneviève Library, Labrouste subjected new techniques to the requirements of a traditional style. Very often, new means are used in this way to serve imaginary schemas or forms from the past. Are such technological anachronisms wrongheaded or fruitful? There is no general answer. Vitruvius maintained that architects invented the layout of stone or marble constructions by imitating the way carpenters assembled pieces of wood for ordinary houses, and this imitation produced the great classical architecture.[29] But Frank Lloyd Wright was harshly ironic about the absurd industrial copies of old artisan forms: plaster cornices, mechanically imitated oriental rugs, painted paper reproducing ancient tapestries, and so on.[30] In opposition to John Ruskin—bane of all modernists—the American architect demands that the new means of construction create forms that suit them and respond to modern needs. It is true that these two examples are not of the same order: Vitruvius's interpretation seems more like a myth than a historical explanation. Wright's criticism suggests that the old forms persist with that much more stubbornness if new processes or materials do not spontaneously engender new forms.

Whatever one says about it, the idea of *forms lagging behind techniques* assumes a valorization of technical progress as well as the idea of an appropriateness of forms to materials. A lack of imagination in the way of applying new expertise is the first reason for the "delay" in the invention of objects or the creation of works. Thus Siegfried Gidion considers that it often takes eighty years for a new principle to find its application, for example, for iron columns and girders to be used in the first skyscrapers or for Volta's discovery of galvanic electricity to lead to the first transfer of electrical energy.[31] But social resistance to innovation is all the more important as it affects the forms. We might wonder, therefore, whether our aesthetic habits—or, in other words, our attachment to forms—don't encourage repetition as much as our technical and gestural habits do.

That is why the tenacity of "aesthetic" criteria is expressed, again in architecture, by the separation between new construction techniques and old "decorative schemas," that is, by the distinction between the "skeleton" and the "dressing" of a building. As we know, even the Eiffel Tower, which we might believe was reduced to a naked structure, was "dressed" by the architect Stephen Sauvestre, who attached great arches to the ground floor, totally useless for construction purposes but aesthetically necessary to make the plans for the tower acceptable in that era. Where did this need for the arches come from? Not from some absolute formal criterion, of course, but from an aesthetic habit supported by old construction techniques. These false arches gave the spectator an impression of stability. The decorative artifice allowed the tower to disguise its modernity with the help of an old costume. In this compromise, a previously functional form survives as ornament, producing a stylistically heterogeneous construction marked by anachronism. In this case, note that the surviving relic claims to draw from "art," whereas the innovation is located on the side of technique.

Moreover, it was established "artists" who, in the name of art and French taste, "protested" to the director of works for the 1887 Exposition against the construction of the "useless and monstrous" Eiffel Tower. "Is the city of Paris going to be associated for years to come with the baroque, mercenary fantasies of a machine builder, making it irreparably ugly and dishonoring it?" protested the prestigious signatories.[32] The engineer responded that the tower would have "its own beauty," since with the curve of its four edges, it would have found the means to resist the wind.[33]

Thus it is not surprising that in 1889, Octave Mirbeau lamented a certain delay of art behind techniques and industry:

> While art seeks intimism and lingers over old formulas, standing about, self-conscious and timid, its gaze forever turned toward the past, industry marches ahead, explores the unknown, conquers the forms ... . It is not at all in the workshops of

painters and sculptors that the revolution, so predicted and so desired, is being prepared. It is in the factories.[34]

In short, Mirbeau observed that art was in the process of becoming anachronistic.

Artists were not the only ones to exclude technical modernity, not just from art, but, more generally, from culture. And not until Gilbert Simondon came along would a philosophical reflection on technical culture be developed.[35]

Aesthetic Fixation

The relationship between the development of techniques and of forms is often expressed by opposing technical value to artistic value, thus assigning a conservative role to art. As artificial as this opposition may be, it works, especially since art is defined as the autonomous domain of forms and the pleasure that they provide. Even outside the strictly artistic field (if such a thing exists), we can observe in fashion, furniture, or useful objects the force of taste that binds societies, groups, or individuals to certain forms, to the point of faithfully reproducing them or preventing their transformation.

Resistance to new forms could be described as the effect of an emotional attachment to forms, as this fixation, or aesthetic habit, is able to contradict the development of new technical possibilities. Forms and techniques are not modified at the same speed as if one were more stable, less changeable than the other. Suppose that the attachment to forms and the difficulty we feel in accepting new ones, as much in the arts as in other areas, are not unrelated to what Freud defines as libidinal fixation (*Fixierung*), indicating by that the attachment to individuals or to "prototypes" leading a subject to reproduce a past method of satisfaction.[36]

Amorous and aesthetic tastes have something in common in that they seek out certain types of objects to love (individuals,

1. Anonymous, *Group of students with their model*,
ca. 1890–1900. Aristotype, 24.6 × 34.2 cm.
École nationale supérieure des beaux-arts, Paris.

2. Oscar Gustav Rejlander, *The head of Saint John the Baptist*, 1856.
Print on albuminated paper using two negatives,
10.7 × 15.1 cm. Royal Photographic Society, Bath.

3. William Lake Price, *Robinson Crusoe and Friday*, 1855–56.
Print on albuminated paper, 25 × 30 cm. Private collection.

4. Julia Margaret Cameron, *King Ahasuerus and Queen Esther*, 1865.
Print on albuminated paper, 31.7 × 27.1 cm. National Museum of
Photography, Film and Television, Bradford.

5. Julia Margaret Cameron, *Saint Agnes*, 1864.
Print on albuminated paper, 27 × 20 cm. National Museum of
Photography, Film and Television, Bradford.

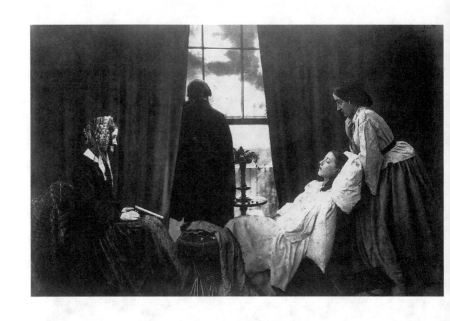

6. Henry Peach Robinson, *Fading Away*, 1858.
Print on albuminated paper using five negatives,
23.8 × 37.9 cm. Royal Photographic Society, Bath.

7. Oscar Gustav Rejlander, *The Wayfarer*, 1858–59.
Print on albuminated paper using several negatives,
26 × 18 cm. National Museum of Photography,
Film and Television, Bradford.

8. David Octavius Hill and Robert Adamson,
The Irish harpist Patrick Byrne in a tableau after Walter Scott's
"The Lay of the Last Minstrel," 1845. Print on salted paper,
21 × 15 cm. Scottish National Portrait Gallery, Edinburgh.

9. Eugène Durieu, *Models posing for Delacroix*, 1854.
Print on salted paper after negative paper, 16 × 12.5 cm.
Bibliothèque nationale de France, Paris.

10. Eugène Durieu, *Studies of model*, ca. 1854.
Prints on albuminated paper after collodion glass negative.
Left, 19.8 x 14 cm. *Right*, 16.5 × 12.3 cm.
Bibliothèque nationale de France, Paris.

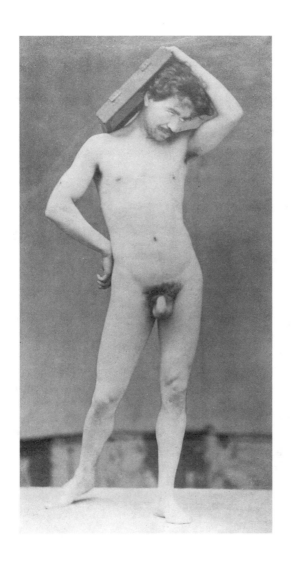

11. Gaudenzio Marconi, *Academic study*, 1870.
Print on albuminated paper, 26.4 × 14.4 cm.
Musée Rodin, Paris.

12. Anonymous, *Models posing for Falguière's*
"Cain and Abel," ca. 1876. Print on albuminated paper,
22.6 × 14.6 cm. Musée Rodin, Paris.

style, forms . . .) and that they must encounter these "objects" (in the broad sense of object of satisfaction) in reality. For Freud, the libido is mobile—he speaks of its "free mobility" (*freie Beweglichkeit*)—because it is capable of passing easily from one object to another. But in other respects it is liable to fixing itself on certain objects or types of objects, thus demonstrating its rigidity or its viscosity (*Klebrigkeit*).

This rigidity is harmful when it fixes desire to lost or past objects, preventing it from turning toward the present, that is to say, available reality. By becoming attached exclusively to an object from the past, in a "fidelity to its investments," the libido deprives itself of the possibility of being satisfied with present objects. This is why for psychoanalysis, fixation is an "anachronism." The idea of fixation here expresses the libido's maladjustment to real changes (as well as an arrest in a developmental process). The double nature of the libido, simultaneously mobile and rigid, forms what Freud defines as its plasticity (*Plastizität*).

Couldn't we say that our artistic tastes demonstrate a similar plasticity? Like our amorous inclinations, aren't they capable of passing from one object to another, from one form to another, and also of solidly attaching themselves to "types" to the point of rejecting any new form?

The ambivalence of this plasticity is exactly what we find again in the two faces of habit. After rereading Aristotle, Catherine Malabou summarized them in this way: "Habit implies the ability to change and the possibility of preserving the modifications inherent in this change."[37] Thus habit is necessarily ambivalent. It has a fundamental value, since we find there the principle for all learning or training. But at the same time as it allows one to acquire competence, it leads to a less positive form of fixation, since it acts as a resistance to new acquisitions or changes.

If we call emotional attachment to forms *aesthetic fixation*, beyond any theoretical or practical interest they hold, this fixation probably presents the same drawbacks as the one described by Freud: the risk of rigidity and maladjustment to reality, the risk of anachronism—of perseverance or maladjustment. It can have the same origin, that is, of depending on early impressions. Far from appearing to us for what it is, the aesthetic fixation often exerts itself in the guise of a defense of things themselves or their concepts. *We often believe we are defending an idea in wanting to preserve a form.*

For example, a powerful viscosity is present in linguistic forms, which fix thinking into old formulas by believing they express eternal truths. In reality, the relationship between form and content or between concept and image is more a matter of a simple "attachment," because it is always in a form that a thought manifests itself. Ideas and concepts do not exist independently of the forms that differentiate them from each other, even if they are only verbal forms.

A remark like Gombrich's about the formation of images illustrates the closeness between concept and image mentioned earlier with regard to images-schemas. The author of *Art and Illusion* proposes that even when an artist claims to imitate a model, he does not begin from a "visual impression" but "from an idea or a concept."[38] The idea or the "concept" here is not some abstract and purely intelligible thing; it already is a form, an image type, a sort of stereotype, a schematized form. Although the "concept" comes to condition and "inform" the artist's perception (in such a way that the artist never draws exactly what he sees), it is already the trace of an old form. For example, an anonymous sixteenth-century German represents the Saint-Ange Castle in Rome as looking like a Germanic castle "with its wood framework and its sloping roofs." An engraver from the same period draws grasshoppers (*Heupferd* in German, literally, "hay horse") by giving them the traits of a strange sort of horse, as if the formation of the image imitated the formation of the word, itself associated with an initial schema. According to Gombrich, the more un-known a thing is—or, indeed, even meaningless—the more it will be represented by identifying it with a known object, that is, with an image type taking the place of the unknown form.

The image type, we must stress, is not derived. It is not the re-sult of an operation of abstraction beginning with the perception of the model; rather, it is the *point of departure* for the imitation, with the artist then completing his drawing according to this or that detail observed from the model.

These examples mean that from the outset, an imaged experi-ence structures thought, competing with the perception and the word, and that aesthetic fidelity binds us solidly to known, habit-ual forms, immediately giving a perceptible content to concepts—at least to empirical concepts. They come to inhabit the imagina-tion and to condition perception itself. Thus representations, including mental images, originate in a legacy of forms to which we are accustomed, indeed even in clichés or commonplaces, so already they inhere in both images and everyday experience. In this sense, imaged experience conditions and sustains the imagi-nation in the same way as lived or "immediate" experience does.

For art history, then, the difficulty is taking into account the transformation of modes of representation, forms, and styles even while fixation is a factor of stability and tradition, indeed even survival. Even when producing useful objects, there is a tendency to give old forms to new objects: the first automobiles resembled carriages or hackney cabs; the first televisions resembled radios, with a screen added on; the icons displayed at the top of comput-er screens always represent the action of "cutting" with scissors and of "opening" a "file" with a cardboard folder. These formal relics range far beyond the domain of artworks—and conversely, it would be hard to restrict any questions of art and its history to the phenomena of aesthetic fixation. Nevertheless, one suspects that fixation plays a role when it is paradoxical or stands in the way of transformations or innovations that seem necessary. Of course, the new is never self-evident, and most of the time, it is afterward, after a laborious process of trial and error, that it becomes clear what forms were more or less suitable. In this case, suitability is not a matter of a judgment of pure taste, in the Kantian sense (that is, bearing only on the *form* of the representation), but a judgment of *applied* taste, that is, bearing on the relationship between a representation and its means, between a work and its medium, between a form and a function. Thus, the fixation with forms can be powerful enough to make a technique as novel as photography trying at first to imitate painting instead of exploring its own possibilities.

A technique like photography, capable of producing images without the mediation of thought, seems, a priori, free of any conceptual authority or aesthetic fixation. Indeed, through its indexical exactitude, through its way of imaging beginning with prints (which makes photos comparable to "casts of nature"),[39] it was able to shatter and to reveal, a posteriori, the formal constraints inherent in the plastic arts by demonstrating how until then our representations owed as much to constructed and transmitted schemas as to pure observation. In the arts, transformations take place more by widening the gaps between existing processes and forms than by returning to a perceived world.

Nevertheless, photography's autonomy in relationship to perception and thought was not enough to let it totally escape certain aesthetic viscosities, as we shall see.

Photographing the Past

The photographs of "*tableaux vivants*" from the Victorian period[40] offer an interesting example of a *weak—even faulty—anachronism* because they maintain pictorial models, that is, because of the discrepancy between their medium and their style. They also illuminate certain artists', notably Baudelaire's, rejection of photography. Finally, they show how artistic intention—the desire to "make art"—can tend toward academicism. It is possible that what we call art never reveals itself as such at the moment when it appears—whether it names objects that have other purposes *after the fact* or whether, and this amounts to the same thing, it is *not yet* recognized in objects for which the social purpose and technical means are new, as was the case for photography and the cinema.

The "*tableaux vivants*" shown at the Orsay Museum testify to the inverse of an artistic claim that betrayed its own medium, instead serving photography, since the "camera" was used to produce the "tableaux."[41]

Let us look at a few of these works: *The Head of Saint John the Baptist*, photographed by Oscar Gustav Rejlander in 1856, was obviously inspired by pictorial representations in both subject and style (illustration 2).[42] If the image here tries to emulate a painting, the subject is most often a literary one. Assisted by his cameraman, David Octavius Hill made a "tableau" of Sir Walter Scott's *The Abbot* (1845–46); William Lake Price photographed *Don Quixote* and *Robinson Crusoe and Friday* (1855–56) (illustration 3); and Henry Peach Robinson photographed *Little Red Riding Hood* in 1858. Julia Margaret Cameron, the most famous and the most interesting of these "pictorialists," photographed *Queen Henriette Marie* in 1874 (announcing their father's death to her children), *King Ahasuerus and Queen Esther* (illustration 4) in 1865, and *Beata* and *Saint Agnes* in 1864, for which she had her pretty servant pose (illustration 5).

If all these images "resemble" tableaux in composition and subject, they strike us no less immediately as photographs. More accurately, the impression they produce is that of neither a photograph nor a tableau but very much that *of a photograph imitating a tableau*. The effect is one of a forgery and not, as their creators hoped, of a photographic fiction capable of competing with painting.

Let us note that before being photographed, *tableaux vivants* constituted a distraction for aristocratic circles. It was a matter of representing a famous pictorial work by reconstructing the scene with the help of individuals disguised and positioned in appropriate scenery—and the guests might be made to guess the subject of the tableau. Goethe gives an example of this practice in *The Elective Affinities* (the heroes must represent Poussin's *Esther Before Ahasuerus*). George Eliot's heroine in her novel *Daniel Deronda* appears in a tableau inspired by Shakespeare's *The Winter's Tale*. Thus literature, along with painting and history, is a source of inspiration for these representations. As a parlor game, the "*tableau vivant*" offers a specific case of a transfer of forms or of style. First, it imitates painting by representing a fixed scene composed as a "tableau," but it also borrows its medium from the theater (employing live actors or walk-ons), and its subjects, from literature and history. Finally, photography brings to these living representations an additional medium by producing the enduring, material, image of the "tableau." The image then supplants the simple parlor game and becomes the object of an artistic ambition entirely on its own. With their own means, the artist-photographers, too, claim to create fictions, symbolic or allegorical figures.

These English ancestors of pictorialism understood how to play on the two tableaux, using the realistic effects of the photographic recording process to better present the imaginary, the dream, or the allegory, relying on objectivity to serve subjective expression and combining the appearance of the real with the expression of the ideal. Photography was reproached for its realism. It wanted to demonstrate that it was capable of producing fictions, to illustrate in its turn the classic imagination.

Of course, this was also what the cinema would try to do—and succeed. But the cinema could achieve its goal only by inventing a

new way of acting or representing, by creating its own style, re-
nouncing the pictorial and theatrical conventions that it had initially imitated, and not without occasional successes. But the
medium is not transparent: it produces effects of which another
medium would not be capable.

Henry Peach Robinson's "tableau" entitled *Fading Away*
(1858) (illustration 6) could almost be an image from film (a pho-
togram). But then again, it could not be: it is too fixed, still dominated by a pictorial *mimesis*. In his *Art of Photography*, it did not
escape Disderi that the living tableau was an "impossible art" and
that the awkward air of the walk-ons made one smile. In 1863,
Thomas Sutton himself recognized that allegorical photography
was a dead end:

> You can choose a beautiful young woman, envelop her artfully
> in bedclothes, make her take a sensuous pose, arrange her slen-
> der fingers delicately and call it "Summer," but it is wasted ef-
> fort, Monsieur Rejlander: this young woman is not Summer. It
> is quite obvious that her name is Jane Brown or Sophia Smith,
> and that the drapery is only bedclothes.[43]

Why can't photographed "bedclothes" be transformed into
"drapery"? Because the photograph *idealizes nothing*. It has the
policelike cruelty of all imprints: it emphasizes the singularity of
things or faces. Thus it inevitably disappoints artistic expectations
of the ideal or the universal—that is, "truth"—that was fundamental to classical *mimesis*. The photographed faces of "Jane
Brown" or "Sophia Smith" are the traces of actual particular ex-
istences and not the image of ideas or of imaginary figures. That
is why Cameron's *Saint Agnes* (illustration 5) or Rejlander's *The
Wayfarer* (illustration 7) seem like failures. The definite article in
the title (*The Wayfarer*) betrays its author's intention, that is, his
desire to represent the *idea* of the wayfarer, according to the clas-

sic pictorial plan. But the man who poses here, caught in his singularity, cannot represent "the" ideal wayfarer. The case of *Saint Agnes* poses the same problem. You could paint an *imaginary* Saint Agnes, but if you photographed her, she would become a *false* saint, because the photo would no longer be a representation in the pictorial sense, that is, an *imitation*.

It is difficult to say whether philosophy imposed its definition of the true on art or art's modes of representation inspired philosophy's conception. But since Artistotle's *Poetics*, ancient *mimesis* required the image to imitate the true in the universal sense, hence the ideal, and never to faithfully reproduce the appearance of a particular object. Classical representation does not model itself on perceptible reality as it is or as it changes, but on a lasting and perfect truth. The challenge for painting and classical art had not only been to "copy" actual appearances but, beyond that, to devise a kind of perfection that nature had not completely realized. In the sixteenth century, the Italian sculptor Vicenzo Danti emphasized the difference between *ritrarre*, "copying faithfully," and *imitare*, "imitating the real to bring it to perfection."[44] Quatremère de Quincy elaborated on this same distinction between "to copy" and "to imitate": going beyond the empirical or "local" model, the artist had to paint according to an ideal model that existed nowhere and that he himself had to create.[45] Thus pictorial representation comes up against the difficulty of reconciling the exactitude of the image and the representation of the idea or the meaning. Photography snaps that ambition in two by capturing precisely the naked appearance—perceptible singularity that nothing transcends, stripped of ideality. We have at our disposal photographs of Saint Theresa of Lisieux, and her smiling face offers us not the slightest *idea* of her piety.[46] But if Theresa is not *the image of her own saintliness*, the portrait can no longer claim to reconcile the physical and the moral resemblance, to combine the exactitude of the appearance and the expression of the ideal. That is why painting has abandoned the portrait, whereas the latter changes in style and meaning with the photograph, and in the arts the self-portrait devotes itself to completely other means.

But it is not so much the timeless as nostalgia for the past that inspires David Wilkie Wynfield when he makes portraits or self-portraits in the dress of the Tudor period. Despite the novelty of his technical apparatus, Wynfield is not oriented toward his time or his contemporaries. Aesthetically, he remains attached to old styles and subjects because they are old: he applies the taste of English romanticism to photography.

How does one reconcile romanticism and photography? By trying to *photograph the past*. That was very much what David Octavius Hill sought, who wrote regarding his Irish harpist (illustration 8): "The photograph of the harpist, whose costume is made up of a blanket and a lap robe, shows how easily one can obtain images of the past."[47] There can be no better expression of the now doubly "anachronistic" conception of photography: its implausible hope of going back in time (to obtain images of the past)—but also, in this case, its out-of-sync nature, turning its back on its time and the possibilities of photography.

This paradoxical project undoubtedly defies common sense, as much as if one wanted to photograph the future. But even though a "subject" that is not before the lens obviously cannot be photographed, why can't photography "represent" or illustrate the past, as do fictional novels, historical films, and photo romances?

The photo serves fiction badly because we know how it is produced. Of course, pictorialism has always practiced fiction, especially in using techniques of collage, superimposition, and superimpression, that is, in modifying the process and even in adding manual interventions. However, as a print of what was actually in front of the camera, a photo is, by nature, documentary. It refers to a thing just as a shadow indicates the reality of an object, because we know how a shadow is created (contrary to the prisoners in Plato's cave who can see only shadows because they cannot look behind themselves). Knowledge of the photographic device makes the photograph proof, in our eyes, of the existence of a "this" that was there, in front of the lens. As Roland Barthes put it, "From a phenomenological point of view, in Photography, *the power of authentication prevails over the power of representation.*"[48] Just as fiction has no need of authenticity because in representation, everything can be feigned, so authentication parasitizes fiction. The scenery for a film does not need to be authentic (you can simulate the Hôtel du Nord or the Pont Neuf . . .), but it would be absurd to photograph scenery to illustrate a history of the streets of Paris.

This power of authentication is the basis for various uses of the photographic process with its variable techniques: scientific[49] or police investigations, marketing information, and, above all, reporting, whose very name perfectly describes the essence of the photographic. The photo has become the privileged medium for every type of identification.

Of course, this principle of authenticity does not prevent the indexical image from being able to preserve the imprint of a fake or a fiction—for example, I can always photograph a false gendarme or scenery. The fake or the fiction, in this case, does not describe the image but the use of the image and, consequently, its legend and its context. The image of the false gendarme is a lie only if the legend presents it as true. It is always conventional devices that establish a fiction as such.

So why couldn't our Victorian photographs be compared with fictions just as photo romances or historical films are? Perhaps because, for a single photograph, the indexical function dominates. It is a simple presentation (for example, of a thing or a face). A man's photograph tells me only that this face exists or that it existed thus, as if I passed him on the street. The truth of the image is existential here in the sense that it indicates an existence and shows that something is, simply, there.

Fiction, on the contrary, leaves suspended the question of existence or makes use of it in some way. A single photograph can function as a fiction only with the help of a legend or a composition (linking together images themselves or texts and images): the syntax of images for a photo romance, the montage of scenes for film, and so forth. Unlike photographed subjects, the actors give living form to the fiction (to the plot or story represented), but as specific individuals, they themselves are discrete elements of the film, in the same way as the scenery and the music are.

Theatrical or cinematic representation uses the physical existence of the actor but does not refer to him—his personal history, his health, his feelings, and his social standing are of no importance to the representation. The audience never believes that Gérard Depardieu or Kevin Costner, or any other actor, *are* the characters they play. Reversing Barthes's formula, we could say that in film, the power of representation prevails over the power of authentication. First of all, the actor is identified as such, that is, considered in his representative function, with his actor's protean nature, his skill at metamorphosis. The audience loves this intermediary being that the professional actor is for them. It is mainly to see him again—always the same and always different—that the audience goes to the show. Regrettable as this may be, it is nevertheless the case. Even before performing a play or acting in a film, the actor and actress are already chimeras, figures situated between the real and the imaginary to which they will give living form. Thus, the famous actor is regarded in three ways simultaneously: as a star, a constructed public figure already "ideal" in terms of his type and style; as a fictional character in terms of his role; and, finally, in the background, as a private individual, a simple mortal in terms of his particular existence. The audience does not confuse these three planes, knowing that the actor they are going to see perform is already an intermediary being, removed from the ordinary world, a sort of blurred synthesis of the roles that he has played.

The photographic image is therefore simply "existential" and signifies no more than the photographed subject. It is materialist in principle, since it preserves only the traces of the visible. That does not render it incapable of truth. But the truth of which this image is capable, outside the systems in which it can play a part, is the disclosure of the particularity, the contingency, the finitude, and the fragility of things.

Through the exactitude of its imprints, photography analyzes the image a posteriori, that is, divides the old pictorial *mimesis* into two distinct functions, an indexical function in which the value of the imprint comes first and an "imaginary" function in which the idea or the dream comes first—breaking the close bonds between image and imagination. The frequent collaboration early on in photography between two individuals[50] reveals this dual function. A "cameraman" for the technical part and an "artist" for the aesthetic part join forces, as if art could be separated from its execution. Hence the artist was the director of the "tableau," a holdover from the time when these scenes were not photographed. It falls to him to *imagine* the scene. The cameraman is in charge of the technical execution of the image. The result is a divorce between the artistic intention and its means, and in the end, these images of individuals who are clearly disguised, a little ridiculous, and who fail to illustrate anything other than themselves.

That being the case, pictorialist and romantic photography allow us to better understand the sarcastic remarks of Baudelaire, who could have witnessed comparable attempts in Paris: "By combining and grouping scamps and hussies, gotten up like the butchers and laundresses at the carnival, by urging these *heroes* to try very hard to maintain the appropriate facial expression for the time needed for the procedure, one claims to render scenes, tragic or graceful, from ancient history."[51] Baudelaire was not wrong. It is true that a great number of these attempts are an insult to "both the divine art of painting and the sublime art of the actor." But if it seems legitimate to denounce an inappropriate style, is it necessary to arrogantly ignore a medium whose future we cannot understand? Baudelaire lets himself be blinded by two debatable and symmetrical conceptions: one that encourages painting to imitate photography and the other that wants photography to imitate painting (as certain "failed painters" then tried to prove by becoming photographers). Neither of these conceptions is satisfactory, since they both ignore the specific link between any given art and its means. Instead of investigating the specific qualities of the two media, Baudelaire remains fixed on painting as the only proper way of making images. Thus he cannot even pose the question of photography.

At the same time, modernity's poet does not want to see how painting is turning, in its own way, toward the present. He is fixed not only on an art but also on a "style." Romantic painting—the model for him of the art of his time—inspires a definition that prohibits any allegiance between art and the present reality. According to him, the artist always imagines more than he observes, or even, as with Delacroix, he imagines what he observes. For him, it is not a matter of seeing but of dreaming in accordance with a nostalgic relationship to the present itself: "Day by day art diminishes its self-respect, groveling before external reality, and the painter becomes more and more inclined to paint not what he dreams but what he sees."[52] Of course, the painter never represents what he sees, since he is always haunted by old images. But the coming of photography abruptly demystified the dream and the imaginary by exposing the world to the harsh light of day and driving the images out of the old frameworks of art.

Existence Caught in the Act

Now let us look at other photos from the same period. In them, we recognize the particular power of an emerging art at the moment when it is not yet concerned about being one.

These are photographs of nudes taken in studios.[53] Simple work aids for painters and sculptors, these photos of living models were meant to replace long posing sessions. Thus they do not take the place of the painting but of the models. Just as the so-called *tableaux vivants* seem like *tableaux morts* today, neither photographs nor paintings, strange but empty, so too these studio photos seem modern. This is because their status as tool, as pure medium, frees them from art and reveals photography to be an observation technique.

For a long time, as we know, photography's status was ambiguous. Even considered as a simple servant to art, its distinction from drawing remained vague. A hierarchy was established between two productions of images that for all intents and purposes were comparable: one artistic and manual, the other industrial and mechanical. Language offers proof of this by the way in which it accommodated photography by applying to it the traditional vocabulary of painting. Thus in 1855, Delacroix says in his journal with regard to photographs *"après"*[after] nude men: "I look at these photographs after nude men passionately and tirelessly, this admirable poem, this human body from which I learn to read, the sight of which says more to me than all the inventions of scribblers."[54] Aside from the criticism of logocentrism expressed by the allusion to a "reading" eye that prevails over the prattle of "scribblers," the expression *"photographies d'après des hommes nus"* does not surprise us. The painter Gérôme used the same phrase: "Dear Monsieur Nadar, would you have the goodness to send me two photographs after Madame Leroux?"[55] Thus the expression was standard. This way of speaking constitutes a linguistic anachronism: for a certain time, language keeps using those forms that have lost or changed their meaning. Likewise, a photograph of a nude model was called a "nude study" or a "human study," according to the terms usually describing preliminary drawings. Reusing these linguistic forms indicates that photos were delegated to the genre of "preliminary work"—without particular concern for the novelty of the process or their possible artistic status—if we exclude photographers like Eugène Derieu, who consciously created demanding works (illustration 10). But the expression "photograph after someone" expresses a second anachronism, that is, the fixed idea of the drawing as the only "model" of image. Nobody today would speak of photos *after* someone, because we grasp them immediately as signs, as traces of the beings themselves—even if it means risking another confusion and believing that the photo could "reproduce" the reality.[56] Thus we forget that it is an image and overlook the specific "indexical" distinction.

This negligence stems especially from a confusion between ordinary perception and the perception of an image, although the immediate experience of the real is never that of an image. The perceived world does not refer back to something else for which it is the image—I see a table, and not the image of a table—any more than it has the physical qualities of an image.

In his *Dictations to Waismann and for Schlick*, Wittgenstein analyzes the difference between lived experience and the observation of images. He notes that the so-called visual image has none of the kind of precision that a material image can have.[57] But neither is it vague: we call it vague or rough in comparison with a photographic image. In fact, it is not a matter simply of an image.[58] On the contrary, the photo constitutes a novel means of seeing, a technique for observing. Moreover, any material image is limited, framed, in relationship to an outside, even if, as Wittgenstein stresses, "one does not see the edges of the visual field."[59] In this way, the framing would be a condition of the image, as with any representational or fictional space, while the real world would be the one lacking any definable edges. That is why illusion presumes that the representation's framework is erased or forgotten. Recall that the prisoners in Plato's cave take the shadows for the things themselves because their field of vision is limited to the wall at the back of the cave. Through this allegory, Plato invites us to consider beyond the frame of our own world, that is, to *imagine* ourselves as the prisoners in the framework of their cave. But this allegorical scene constitutes a metaphysical trap, because there is no "framework" that we can leave (unlike the prisoners) to go beyond this world. Such are the confines specific to modern thought: to consider that neither metalanguage nor metavision exists, but only the visible field in which everything is real, everything is shadow—which amounts to the same thing. The world is not a cave because it has no outside: end of allegory and thus of metaphysics.

Let us return to the painters' studio. At first glance, the impression produced by studio photographic nudes is not totally different from that of the photos with "artistic" pretensions: they present the same ambiguity, the same strangeness, because the models here are posing *before* a photographer but *for* the painter or sculptor. The poses are intended for the representation, whereas the scenery and the props are those of the studio, not the painting. The photo, however, "takes" it all: the model, flesh and bone, with his ostentatious pose and the corner of the studio that serves as "background" to the image. As scenery for the photo, the studio is the *reverse side of the scenery* for the painting: photography takes art *in reverse*.

The photographic "model," who imitates in advance the painted character for whom he serves as a model, clearly cannot embody the ideal the painter dreams of—no more than the young women that Julia Margaret Cameron photographed could embody madonnas. But our studio models do not have such pretensions, and these photographs—which were taken until the twentieth century—are not meant to be regarded as tableaux. Moreover, photography does not spare us the tattoos and hair follicles of the Italian model,[60] the ordinary lines of a face, or the scaffolding, the threadbare rugs, the various bedclothes—those again—meant to imitate drapery and make us forget the coarseness of these places. Thus, it is against this prosaic, everyday background that the model feigns noble gestures and tries to strike heroic postures.

If they are viewed through the eyes of a lover of paintings, these photographs could be disappointing or amusing. Observed with a modern eye, used to an aesthetic of the instantaneous, we find them equally disconcerting for their hybrid character—as if, here again, we perceive a time lag between the style and the medium of the image. The artistic intention still appears in the pictorial pose, but the images present individuals as they are, more or less beautiful, with their accompanying characteristics.

These shots thus become fascinating for the shift in perspective that they require of us. At the very moment that this nude body fails to illustrate an idea, to tell a great story, to represent some mythic hero, the simple trace of its existence astonishes and moves us. The universal is lacking, but an absolutely singular existence is substituted for the old expectation. It presents itself before our eyes and requires that it be seen as it is, in all its imperfect and finite reality.

Without trying to produce a work of art, the photographer has surprised his "models," *catching them in the act of existence.* Constructed as tableaux or allegories, the photos reveal the singularity of human bodies whose nudity, harshly exposed, appears in all its prosaic truth.

Neither Gaudenzio Marconi's academic study (illustration 11) nor the two men, one holding the other on his shoulder, photographed for Falguière's *Cain and Abel* in about 1876 (illustration 12) give us a glimpse of any mythic figure. These are men made nude, exposed, in the simplicity of their vulnerable, carnal existence. This existence presents itself before our eyes, canceling out all symbolic significance. Aside from aesthetic effect, unintentional absurdity, or obscenity, that is what finally makes these images impressive to us or, as Barthes would say, *poignant*. These strange characters, who still evoke the abolished or suspended time of the pictorial aesthetic, refer here to the *present* of the photographic imprint, plunging our vision into an anachronistic vertigo.

At the moment when it thinks it is serving what was the classical beauty of drawing or when it contributes to art's effort to measure up one last time to the timeless ideal, studio photography reveals, without wanting to, the finitude of modern man. It restores him to his own time, that is, to his passing and uncertain being. It presents the image of a frailty that we can no longer conceal from ourselves.

Political Time

. . . . .

PATIENCE AND DEMOCRACY

· · · · ·

DEMOCRACY is always a matter of *temporizing*. It cannot be conceived of without this continual obligation to *take the time*—to develop proposals, to discuss the possible options, to persuade, to implement decisions. Democratic power is always exercised more slowly than individual authoritarian power. Thus democracy must remain patient, even at those times when it encounters, more or less fortunately, the media's haste.

The *impatience* of the media and the *patience* of democracy are therefore the causes of a certain number of *contretemps* between politics and the media. But there may also be other differences of opinion, especially regarding the role of public opinion, which I will consider first.

Political life cannot be separated from the areas in which public opinion is expressed or measured. Whether or not we would like to, political representation cannot be isolated from the theater of public opinion because democracy is made up of concrete procedures according to which its real power is linked to the supreme authority, the people, and, in an indirect way, to what is called public opinion. Those procedures, which can be very different depending on the period and the nation, are much more than simple forms: in concrete ways they determine the very contents of the concept of democracy.

Actually, what the supreme authority thinks, feels, and desires must truly be able to be presented and represented. Thus the citizens' connection to power manifests itself simultaneously through voting and public opinion, and it would be strange to maintain that the people can express themselves only by voting. Even if the political will as such is expressed in political institutions by representatives of the people, the democratic debate also takes place in the public space, and it overflows the political arena in the narrow sense. The whole problem lies in the way these two spaces are both distinct and interfere with each other in modern democracies. In a little city-state where "direct" democracy would be possible, the public space and the political space would be one and the same: the citizens could gather, debate, and decide within a single and identical assembly on a single and identical stage. Thus there would be no reason to distinguish, from within, public opinion from political will. One would lead to the other. But in a representative democracy, one never deals with the population itself in its entirety. Whether it is a matter of its political will or its opinions, and outside those places where a local democracy can and must be developed, a large population is necessarily represented or symbolized. Those who express themselves in various public situations give a face to public opinion, while the political will is constructed within political institutions *stricto sensu*.

There exists, moreover, a form of "representation" of the people that involves neither public expression nor political representation but, rather, aesthetic visibility: the people want to see themselves. Much more than in the little city-states where they could assemble, the people today need images with which to identify.

That is the purpose, for example, served by demonstrations at the great meetings, shown on the screen, as well as the images of anonymous citizens photographed by the press or interviewed on television stage sets and in the streets.

The public debate is much wider and more open than the institutional political debate, even if it never includes all the citizens. It also takes place according to other rhythms, and public opinion can always enter into conflict with the elected representatives as well as with the government.

Of course, a democracy acknowledges the autonomy of the elected, which should, in principle, shield them from the daily pressures of public opinion. If we do not want the specific nature of politics and its institutions to disappear, its power must remain the decisive authority, and it does not have to follow unconditionally a more or less discernible public opinion.

If public opinion cannot govern, it is also true that when the gaps between public opinion and political power are significant and obvious, they become harder and harder to endure. A "too" profound divide between public opinion and political power is unacceptable and would throw the democracy into a crisis. But how, apart from exceptional situations or violent demonstrations, can a threshold be established beyond which this divorce becomes dangerous or intolerable, and what is it that now gives so much political weight to public opinion? It is the question of time again: the rhythm of electoral consultations often seems too slow to those who confuse the democratic will with the day-to-day feelings of the citizens. The pressure of the everyday, which dominates the press, tends to circumvent political temporality, even though periodic elections attempt to give the floor regularly to the citizenry itself.

The media's expression of public opinion, ultimately broadcast hour by hour, even minute by minute, enters into competition with the real time of political life or the official time of institutions. Where does the responsibility for temporizing public opinion or its effects lie? With politics, no doubt, in the first place, because it is up to politics to demand respect for the political rhythm provided by the institutions or required by events and not to give in to media pressures; but also with the citizens, who must resist the feverish appeal of the media machinery—this is what Americans confronted with the ridiculous "Lewinsky affair" did—and finally with all media professionals if they become aware of their power to regulate how social time is measured and if they also want to act as citizens.

An additional difficulty is that public opinion is never simple. It does not necessarily obey the logic of the experts, economists, or philosophers—any more than it necessarily obeys the logic of the demagogues. Some regard public opinion all the more uneasily, since it extends far beyond the circle of the "educated public," as it used to be called, or the "elite," as is still often used today. Especially frightening is the opinion of the "general public" or, worse, the "masses," who are seen as replacing the former "well-read" and privileged public who, from the Enlightenment until the Third Republic, shaped public opinion. A similar nostalgia for these old "publics" seems to possess theorists as removed from one another as Jürgen Habermas[1] and Régis Debray, the first through the critique of a manipulative mass culture and the second through the critique of a state "humbled by technology" and transformed despite itself into a *seducer state*.[2] If the "democracy of public opinion" is not democracy, neither can the latter want to restrain public opinion or control the places where it is expressed. And as Régis Debray demands, if it is necessary "to reconcile the culture with its materiality,"[3] the issue is not one today of deploring the perverse effects of the media, but of rethinking and especially of revitalizing democracy in the era of its mediatization. An external struggle "against" the media is not possible because there is no longer any exterior—but work on the functioning and the interference of public spaces among themselves is possible and necessary.

Democracy can develop today only with a democratization of the media, beginning with a consideration from within about its cultural and political responsibility in the broader sense and on the basis of genuine *statutes and contracts*, about which citizens ought to be able to express themselves. Nothing should be more responsive to the idea of *public service* than the audiovisual media, but even in France where this concept still means something, the logic of *publicity*, in the commercial sense of the word, seems to have gotten the better of public interest, on the private television channels as well as on the so-called public channels.

Before considering further certain aspects of the media scene, let us look more generally at how the issue of *representation* enters into both the notion of the political and the public scene; in other words, let us examine the status of public opinion.

Political Representation and Its Theater

As early as the seventeenth century, political philosophy experienced the ambiguity of its conception of the people, that is, of a population sometimes perceived and feared as a "multitude," sometimes established as a single unit. It was able to invest political authority in the multitude only by unifying it through its representation. That is why the "multitude" is constituted as a people, *singular*, in Hobbes,[4] by having itself "represented" by a single sovereign, the monarch. According to this first instance of representation in political thought, the sovereign represents the people, just as in the theater, the *persona*, the character, represents the play's author on the stage. As character and "actor,"[5] the monarch acts in the name of the people, his true and invisible author.

The multitude acquires its own identity as a people only if it becomes a *person*, when it is represented by the individual figure of the monarch. This means that the political authority of the people is manifested and disappears simultaneously in the person of the king—the multitude withdraws before the people, itself incarnated in a single person.

Rousseau, who also could not conceive of a divided sovereignty, imagined, with the *general will*, a guarantor principle for the political unity of the people. This fiction of a unique and infallible will, desiring only the general interest, avoids the risk that the conflict of multiple wills and the inevitable divisions between actual citizens, even democratically assembled, would present to the sovereignty of the people. Rousseau knew very well that a real *people*, even assembled, is never *one,* singular. Thus democracy is impossible for the author of the *Social Contract*: it never existed, Rousseau said, "in the strict sense." Any institution, any process, for representing the will of the people is interpreted here as a factor of separation that alters its identity. Any delegation, any representation, is alienating.

But the myth of the individuality of the people, in correlation with the myth of the people's indivisibility, expresses a fixation with a monarchial model according to which the sovereign power *is* a single will. The people seem to be able to be sovereign only if they constitute a single will, hence an individuality.

On the contrary, a consideration of the Greek origins of democracy would confirm that it assumes neither the individualization of the citizens nor the unity of their "will." Political decisions require neither unanimity nor the resolution of conflicts. The city is not a unity but a plurality (*plethos*), just as Aristotle argued against Plato. The only limit to conflict—in a democracy—is a consensus to renounce violence as a way to settle debates. It remains true that a people made up of a large number of individuals can neither deliberate nor decide immediately and directly—except with small local structures—and in this sense, the theater production imagined by Hobbes as the basis for political representation remains inescapable. However, unlike the monarchial "representation" described by Hobbes, the actors on the stage in a democracy are numerous, and the public, in this last case, must remain the author of the play. Under such conditions, it is a matter of not succumbing to the anguish of division and of inventing better means of "representing" a people, who are always, in the end, "unfindable."[6]

From a sovereign people to the reality of power, there is never anything but "representations," or, if we prefer, figures. The political community exists nowhere outside the forms that it makes for itself through its institutions and the individuals who bring them to life. The *distance* between the people and those who represent it cannot be abolished, and any democracy is a way of regulating that distance in such a fashion that the people remain, as much as possible and in reality, the authority out of which a political "will" originates. Naturally, as a way of distancing, political representation is also a way of temporizing. With its rhythm, political temporality cannot coincide with the life and rhythms of society and public opinion. Nevertheless, everything happens as if the actors in a democracy exhaust themselves trying to *synchronize* political life and the life of society—an impossible task.

Thus the way in which a people—by nature multiple and diverse—participates in public and political life is always a matter of a very complex art that is performed on both the public and the political stage. But it is also always a matter of stages and performances establishing their space and their own temporality. Media spaces, the current locales of democratic visibility, are again a matter of a theatrical structure, even if we are dealing with the screen. This structure organizes the "production" of power as much as of public opinion. It is theatrical, essentially and not by accident, because for a people, it is a matter of seeing and hearing itself (of seeing itself govern and hearing itself speak). But no image guarantees the accuracy of the representations (political and media), since it is a figure and not a reflection. It is futile, therefore, to think of being able to leave the theaters of power and public opinion, or the "media scene," if it is only to fall back into the myth of the people's immediate relationship with itself.

The metaphysical idea of a people governing itself without representation would have to assume the existence of a homogenous, even amalgamating, society, protected from conflicts by the obliteration of the political but paving the way for all homogenizing acts of violence. There is never a lack of voices claiming to speak directly in the name of the people. Charismatic and authoritarian power generally presents itself as a privileged "medium" for the people, "directly" expressing the people's will. Thus the "radical" calling into question of representation, even of entertainment, threatens democracy by claiming to accomplish it and by believing it can do without mediations and intermediaries.

Kant's Enlightenment

Before the Revolution, the "public" was never the people, from whom it expressly distinguished itself. More precisely, it defined itself *itself* as the well-read and educated public, distinct from the "multitude" or the "populace." According to Habermas, there long existed a "plebeian public sphere" outside literary space, but it was "repressed" and took up its post, punctually, only with the French Revolution.[7] In fact, Arlette Farge has shown that popular opinion, "officially nonexistent" in the eighteenth century, was treated "with the most extreme attention" by the monarchial power, especially under Louis XV.[8]

Since the seventeenth century, however, the public has been, above all, the arts public. As in antiquity, it is at the theater that public space and the public itself are created (in Greek, the theater first designated not the stage that one watched but the place where one watched from). The public is also the lettered public: the one that reads and often writes, particularly critiques of art and literature. Made up of the whole of those who judge such works, it soon extended its judgments to political life.

Just as in the period when dramatic works became the object of public competitions, we cannot separate the idea of the public from the idea of judgment. The question is to know how to judge in the plural and whether one judges better alone or with others. In the eighteenth century, this becomes linked to the problem of public opinion.

We know that the Age of the Enlightenment valued the "tribunal" of the public sphere to the point of recognizing it as the touchstone for the accuracy and rationality of opinions. In 1784, in *What Is the Enlightenment?* Kant appeals to a "public use of reason,"[9] so that each individual might freely expose his thinking to the test of the judgment of the "public that reads." Is this public use of reason, which involves reasoning before the other, enough to give the Kantian position a political dimension? I believe that is not at all the case and that the "publicity" of this thinking must be given its proper place here.

Kant's progression is political only to the extent that he argues for the freedom of thought. Each individual must be free to think for himself, that is, to make use of his own understanding. The place where this freedom is exercised is in writing or, more precisely, in publication, a space withdrawn from any institutional framework. The importance of publication, according to Kant, is that it escapes all powers, notably the church and the state, in other words, the institutions where speech is inevitably *supervised*. That is why Kant qualifies the use of speech within an institutional framework as "private." Thus this manifesto in favor of the Enlightenment aims at guaranteeing, "for the learned," a place for free reasoning, independent of all powers, offered solely to the judgment of independent readers themselves.

This position was perfectly legitimate. It appeals, as Spinoza had already done, to the freedom of thought, which knows no limits and implies the possibility of expressing one's ideas and knowing those of others. It has lost nothing of its value, especially in light of the contemporary expansion of a "politically correct" ideology, which, in the name of moral or political principles, would like to censor speech and writing.

But in other respects, Kant belongs to another time: whatever one says of them, the thinkers of the Enlightenment only illuminated a world still completely intact under the *ancien régime*. The philosopher awaits the learned, who are supposed to progress together toward a rational and universal thinking, including political matters, about which they enlighten the monarch and peacefully engage him on the path to reforms (that he alone will decide). The well-read and well-to-do public, who is not cold or hungry or angry, is not in any particular hurry: *it has all the time in the world*. It needs only to reason and leaves to the ruling power the responsibility to act when the time seems right. We are not dealing here with a democratic patience but with a wholly aristocratic indifference. A few years after this writing by Kant on the Enlightenment, the French Revolution showed that public opinion, broadened to include the people, entered into a completely different relationship with time.

Considered narrowly, the difference between the learned and the people still exists today, although the "well-read public" is now called "the experts" or "the economists." The theorists take the wrong tack when they forget to include in their calculations—at certain times—the impatience of those who can no longer wait, even if they are not represented on the public or political stage. Democracy betrays itself if it forgets that representation is always insufficient and approximate—and that it is necessarily so. To avoid this oversight is to take into account the people in its entirety, to evaluate its urgent needs, even when they are not yet expressed politically. Thus, democratic patience has its limits.

The conception of free thought in *What Is the Enlightenment?* does not involve a political manner of thinking, and especially not a way of taking opinions into account in a democratic debate, since the free use of reason is reserved for a place (writing) and an elite who can only hope to sway the ruling powers and influence the mind of the people.

Finally, Kant's thinking remains stamped with a very dated idealism if it implies that the public use of reason is enough to favor or to guarantee the expression of a universal truth. Despite its total autonomy, can the learned public embody a universal point of view? Nothing is less certain. It is not enough to reason freely in order to speak in the name of "man." This illusion of universality has been sufficiently denounced to make it necessary to return to it. Let us only say here that while it claims to represent "a universal civil society," in legal and political matters the public in fact identifies its own bourgeois, proprietary, well read, male (and not female) interests that it calls the "universal man's." Moreover, Kant himself shows how specific his "universal man" is: in *The Doctrine of the Law*, he limits the political use of reason—and consequently the citizenship—to property owners only. Those who are not "their own masters"—for example, wage earners, domestics, and women—cannot be citizens. However much Kant wants to establish strict boundaries between public and private uses of reason—as if thinking, by the sole virtue of being written, could extricate itself from any empirical condition—his objects of reflection themselves belong to a very concrete social area, and when he reasons, he clearly cannot abstract himself from his own social condition (as man and university professor).

In a later text,[10] often compared with the previous one, Kant envisages a kind of judgment before human reason as a whole on order to escape the illusions resulting from the empirical existence of each individual. This can be found in those famous passages on "common sense" and "broadened minds" (*erweiterte Denkungsarte*) that require one to think "by putting oneself in the place of the wholly other." Hannah Arendt believed that she detected here the political concern for "sharing the world with others."[11] This interpretation seems to me to "force" the Kantian text. Indeed, note that the others in whose "place" I must put myself for judging are in no way *real* others; it is not to their *actual* judgments that I must subject my thinking but only to their possible judgments—an abstraction made up of empirical contingencies. So then, what is it to put oneself "in the place of the wholly other" if this other is as lacking as I am in particular conditions shaping his judgment, if he is as abstract as I am? The game of substitution becomes absolutely vertiginous: I put myself in the place of the wholly other to know how he would judge if he put himself in the place of the wholly other and so on. We think we are confronted with the other's point of view when in reality, we never leave our place: by rising above subjective conditions for judgment, one "situates" oneself immediately, Kant explicitly states, at a *universal* point of view. Do we think we determine, much less test, this universal by placing ourselves, through our thinking, at the other's point of view? But—and this is the philosophical trap—the other vanishes before this improbable "point of view of the universal" that makes in advance an abstraction of any empirical condition! This point of view of all and of no one as disinterested as my own thus vanishes into a pure place, an empty place. What sense is there in putting oneself in the place of someone who hypothetically is nowhere? "Other" here denotes some transcendental, that is, utopian, subject, and not any such real individuals with their conditions for existence. This is not someone whom I actually should listen to in order to be able to get to know him, and thus an empirical individual; this is an other for whom *I my-*

self construct the abstract and general figure. The political field, conforming to Hannah Arendt's own logic, is not one of such abstract universalism but one of confrontation.

For Arendt, it is a matter of imagining "how I would feel and think" if I were in the place of others. But the major concern she has for impartiality[12] leads to covering all perspectives, not to making an abstraction of them. Political judgment must result from a *synthesis* of particular perspectives, and not from their obliteration.

The Kantian idea of *common sense (sensus communis)*, which claims to make abstractions of particular sensations and emotions and to rise above any subjective point of view, does not constitute a *political* manner of thinking *with* others but, rather, a *philosophical* manner of thinking before a fiction of the other. In Kant, the reference to the other is to an *ideal* otherness and not to an *empirical* otherness. As an abstract universal figure, the other has no relationship to the real existence of others to which politics is related.

But if an actual public is involved, we are dealing with a political judgment in which each individual must take into account all the others and try to come to consensus with them. In this way we can speak of democracy. This is why those who strive to determine the just and the unjust—a political task—cannot confine themselves to the point of view of an abstract universality.

Bergson's Choice

Unlike philosophical radicality and Kantian universality, the true taking into account of others' opinions is the sign of political thinking, as Arendt maintained. In the same period, Maurice Merleau-Ponty went still further in bringing philosophical truth itself back into the world and in searching for it in the heart of events. In his *Leçon inaugurale* at the Collège de France, he declared that "our relationship to the true comes through others,"[13] giving the example of Bergson's decision not to convert to Catholicism; this was in 1937. Despite his personal conviction, aware of the "formidable wave of anti-Semitism that is going to sweep over the world," Bergson rejected converting to Christianity in order to "remain among those who will be tomorrow's persecuted." For the philosopher, it is not simply a matter here of resolving a conflict between individual religious truth and a "political" choice that, taking account of others, prohibits one's desertion from the persecuted's camp. Why should the political prevail over the religious or the philosophical? It is not in terms of conflict but of a more profound synthesis that Merleau-Ponty interprets Bergson's choice and inscribes it within a complex genesis of the truth. This is a truth that, as synthesis, is not a "tête-à-tête between the philosopher and the truth" or the expression of a subjective certitude or the taking into account of others alone. For Merleau-Ponty, a philosophical life cannot abandon any of these three authorities. "Bergson attests," he writes, "that for him there is no *place of truth* where one ought to go to seek it at any cost, even by breaking off human relationships and bonds with life and with history."[14] The problem is one not only of emancipating politics from philosophy, as Arendt rightly did, but also of contesting all transcendence with regard to truth and of affirming in a completely novel way that "the philosophical absolute is to be defended in each instance." Merleau-Ponty completed his lesson by citing these words of Alain's to his students: "The truth is momentary for us humans who have the short view. It is of a situation, an instant; we must see it, speak it, make it at that exact moment, not before or after, in ridiculous maxims; not many times, because nothing is for many times."[15]

It would be nice to remain in the company of such words for a long time and meditate on them each time that the contempt for circumstances or the deceptive rigidity of universal "maxims" threatens us. Being momentary does not render the truth invalid.

It remains requisite at each instant, like synthesis, without certainty, in judging each time without having at one's disposal principles or general laws.[16]

Thus in many ways democracy poses the question of its proper relationship to time. By the simple fact that it is based on representation, it involves procedures and institutions that temporize the expression of the public opinion and the political will.

If it cannot be based on any unconditional truth, political judgment calls for exercising an art of shared, and not solitary, judgment that must employ certain procedures and demands time. Finally, the distinctive feature of democratic representation is that it is essentially *ephemeral*, since the control of power must always come back to the sovereign authority. The only means for not removing sovereignty from the people is to entrust its representatives and its authorities with power that is always *provisional*. This is why democracy has created a new political time, punctuated by elections. This institutional temporality breaks with the political time of monarchial regimes prescribed by the duration of the monarch's life, that is, by the rhythm of the distinction between generations of the royal family. The difference of generations still plays a not inconsiderable role in democracies, no doubt—for example, in political parties—but it is a hidden role, escaping the rules and the official institutional operations.

Today, politics maintains a new relationship to time to the extent that it ceases to refer to an eternal model or a necessary teleological process. Under these conditions, each type of event is inscribed in a particular temporality, and the time scale is not the same for political events as different as a war and an election, an economic event, a transformation in moral standards, a demographic evolution, or a constitutional change. One of the difficulties for contemporary politics is that the rhythm of democratic life does not coincide with that of other movements that articulate the history of societies. But before turning to media time, let us reconsider for a moment the question of judgment and the status of rhetoric.

Politics and Rhetoric

The Greek model of democracy brings into play some procedures that link politics with rhetoric. Let us consider this model for a moment to see how it can enlighten us today.

When the power (*arkhé* ceases to be embodied in one individual and is placed at the center (*méson*) among the citizens, then it becomes a matter of knowing how they are going to share this power and make decisions concerning the public domain, that is, their common interests. The Greek response is an institution utilizing a technique of assembly. Citizens assembled[17] in a single place make judgments about the common good by practicing *public debate* in which the possible choices are presented and argued, and then they vote to adopt a decision. Thus the assembly also uses a *technique of democratic judgment*. On the one hand, debate takes place; on the other hand, so does the vote that allows one position to win over the others. The two moments must be linked: a vote without a debate would be blind, and a debate without a vote would be futile. Aristotle reminds us that it is necessary only to *deliberate*, in the strict sense, if we must *decide*. Indeed, it is by being bound by the decision to follow that deliberation can be made accountable. In having to make a decision for all, each individual tends to think more of the common good. Thus the call for public opinion's responsibility is all the more urgent, since it also must declare itself politically, decide, and hence vote. (Herein lies sufficient reason for increasing the opportunities for polling in our democracies).

The gathering of *all the citizens* into one deliberative assembly always illustrates for us the functioning of an exemplary democracy, as if the Greek city-state ought to remain our political model. This nostalgia for the Greek model sometimes makes it difficult to be resigned to representation—and even more so to the divorce between the public scenes of debate and the political sphere of decision. Nevertheless, the model of a people's assembly, even in a small city, cannot guarantee the absolute validity of decisions, any more than any other form or process can.

The technique of assembly brings to light opinions in all their diversity and undoubtedly allows for the development of a *public* judgment, but even in this case, there are many ways of forming and evaluating this public judgment. Whether the judgment is political or of some other nature, the problem is knowing how to move from the plurality of the judges to the unity of a single decisive judgment. The rule involves taking a majority into account, but it does not necessarily involve a debate.

According to Aristotle, a plurality is a better judge than a single individual *in matters of art and poetry*, because *each individual* judges *one part* according to his individual tastes and abilities, and *all* judge *the whole*. A plurality of viewpoints enriches the overall quality of the judgment (a little like the way the meal is richer and more varied when everyone brings something different to a picnic).[18] Thus the collective judgment here results from the *sum of particular judgments*. Likewise, in politics, the justness of a democratic judgment does not come from the superior competence of each individual (an oligarchic criterion) but from the sum of the "fragments of practical wisdom." The sum of many different viewpoints finally produces a good judgment. The good judgment is in the sum, not in the abstract universality.

This way of understanding public judgment is a little different from the one that requires that an assembly make a judgment at the end of a *debate*. In this case, the principle is really that opinions *mutually correct one another* rather than adding up. Hegel holds, for example, that an assembly must be "a living assembly,

where one is mutually informed and persuaded, where delibera-
tions take place in common."[19]

Even for a *deliberative* assembly, it is still necessary to know at
the end of a debate whether the goal is a *victory* or a *consensus*.
The Greek conception is, rather, one of a polemic followed by a
clear victory, established by a vote.

Finally, the judgment of an assembled public obeys more obscure laws: the contagiousness of emotions and feelings or a
group's tendency toward fusion as it perceives itself and delights
in its unity. Far from being dominated by reason alone, the technique of assembly allows a specific kind of rhetoric to be deployed. It can never rule out any fusing effects or the pleasure of
"forming a body" specific to other types of gatherings—like meetings, festivals, and street demonstrations. In no way does it avoid
collective emotion, and it lets the pressure of the whole on individuals or groups come into play. Hence, the weight of arguments
and reciprocal *exchange* (so dear to Habermas) are not the only
components in the assembly's operation. Any democratic process
has its negative effects. It is because we overlook them that we idealize this or that ancient form or stigmatize the perverse effects of
modern modes of operation, blaming political representation for
never being close enough to the people, and mediatization for
alienating political life.

Guy Debord's critique of the "society of the spectacle,"[20] ap-
pealing for its vigor, is still a critique of representation inspired by
metaphysics. It is a modern version of Rousseau's *Lettre à d'Alem-
bert*, revised and corrected in a neo-Marxist style. For Guy Debord,
representation *distances*, as Rousseau had already said, and the
spectacle threatens to separate and detach what must remain immediate, close to itself, present with itself. The spectacle here is not
what corrupts power by requiring it to be seductive, contrary to its
nature, but what imitates it and carries it out, as if in its religious or
political forms, it had always been the alienating externalization of

human powers. "The spectacle," writes Debord, "is the technical realization of the *exile* of human powers into a beyond."[21] Social, moral, or political evil is in the spectacle because it is, more generally, in the separation, that is, in the representation.

But the spectacle is not "beyond." It takes place at the heart of the social, with the first image that society gives itself of itself, with the first function that it delegates. If it is clear, as we maintain here, that the immediacy and the pure self-presence of the people involve a myth, then institutional representation or the spectacle or the media are not in themselves politically corrupt. They constitute modalities of representation, inescapable and to be judged by measuring their particular effects, good and bad—always both at the same time.

As soon as we enter the domain of fundamental political choices, and thus of the just and unjust, it becomes a question of agreeing on ways to establish common principles. Thus we can no more do without rhetoric than without theater.

When it is addressed to a public it must convince, public speaking can be understood as a technique of *demonstration*, on the one hand, and *persuasion*, on the other. That is not the same thing, as Aristotle shows in his *Rhetoric*. *Demonstration* is a matter of the logic of *the true*: it begins from definite premises and involves the arguments included in the elaboration of a theoretical knowledge. *Persuasion* is a matter of the logic of the *plausible*: it begins from plausible premises (*endoxa*), but not absolutely certain ones, and involves those areas like the legal or the political, where it is a matter of persuading a public that makes judgments. Serving as persuasion, rhetoric seems to involve a purely *partisan* logic (of a client of a party), which explains its bad reputation and makes it as suspect as politics itself.

This harshness would be justified if it were possible in politics to stick to demonstration and refrain from persuasion, in other words, if one could oppose to *political rhetoric* a *political philos-*

ophy based on truth. Such is not the case, despite the desire of the philosophers who, since Plato, have dreamed of founding politics on philosophy. But *for us*, the principles on which democratic political life is founded are no longer a matter of immutable, or even demonstrable, knowledge. In this sense, they make neither metaphysical nor scientific claims. With regard to the principle of equal rights, Arendt justly writes: "That all men are created equal is neither evident nor demonstrable."[22] Equality is not a *truth* in the classic sense; it is a modern principle of which we have mutually convinced ourselves and that we have decided to establish as the foundation of the constitution, in France and in many other democracies. If politics is not based on unquestionable truths, it cannot do without the consent of the people, and persuasion necessarily plays an essential role there. In this sense, as the art of finding the most persuasive arguments on each individual subject, rhetoric is not just the "cynical" means of defending any viewpoint whatever, even counter to the truth, because this "truth" is fundamentally lacking. Neither is it the means of cleverly communicating an accepted truth (even if it can also serve as that): given the necessity of making *choices based on no absolute certitude*, it is already the search for arguments capable of winning the approval of those who make judgments—that is, the citizens. That is why, as Spinoza affirmed, politics must always reckon with their fears and hopes.

Our low regard for rhetoric comes from recognizing only its instrumental role in serving a *preexisting prejudice*, making it a partisan weapon. But if politics is not a science and if decisions are made with uncertainty, then one must persuade oneself just as much as the citizens—and isn't the best argument for convincing others also the one that will best persuade me? In other words, searching for arguments in political matters can serve the victory of my "party," if not my "partiality," just as it can serve, *for myself*, to define, without certitude or evidence, what could win the approval of the majority. Before being the weapon for partisan battles, rhetoric is a tool of persuasion that has its place in the democratic debate; indeed, it is even a process of reflection, a method for testing the "reasons" for a choice *for myself and for others*. Under these conditions, there is no longer any obvious reason for opposing knowledge to art or the rigor of reasoning to the "artifices" of appeal.

MEDIA TIME

. . . . .

Media, the Public, and the Masses

WE NO LONGER oppose the *public* to the *people*, as was done in the eighteenth century, but, according to a basically comparable segregation, the public to the *masses*. On the one side, we wrongly place the "true" public, the cultivated minority; on the other, the "uneducated," undiscerning throngs. These categories seem to echo the disqualification of the audiences of audiovisual mass media.

Could the techniques of communication engender "cultural classes" in the same way as the techniques of production have defined social classes? For those who disqualify them, the *masses* designates in general the immense public that is both *sensitive* and *subject* to the seductiveness of the image, without really knowing if it is sensitive because it is uncultivated or if it is culturally proletarianized by media methods themselves. Perhaps that amounts to the same thing: as soon as we discredit sensitivity a priori and we place the image at the lowest level of culture, the least cultivated *masses* seem more sensitive to images than to concepts. This mythic *mass* that is the "general public" is always being reproached for feeling too much and not thinking enough.

No doubt the "general public" cannot be the measure of artistic values—but no public can be that. The public that is limited to "specialists," the one that willingly considers itself the elite and that in our day ponders earnestly before Jean-Pierre Raynaud's potted plants or Joseph Beuys's rolls of felt, offers no guarantee either, after all. It has its own principles of conformism, and for not being those of the general public, its own market laws are not necessarily better ones. Flattering the taste of the schools and the coteries runs more or less the same risks as wanting to please everyone: there can be as many stereotypes in a "scholarly" artistic production intended for a limited audience as in a work aimed at popular success. (Obviously we are speaking here only of works of art and not narrowly scientific works that are, by nature, meant for specialists.) If the justness of artistic judgments is not guaranteed by a public determinable in advance, artists would do well to maintain some distance from public opinion, at least *while they are working*, since exposure to the public takes place *at another time*. This point could seem in conflict with creative activities in the democratic space, but couldn't political life itself need many different times? A time for private or semipublic work—necessary for studying and developing ideas, for inquiry, for consultation—and a time for the public debate and decision? Where can we find this time if the press and the media claim the right to see and to know without limits and without delays? The demand for continual information in real time and the competition between radio or television channels tend to shrivel up the possibility of nonpublic political work. The distinction between work time and public time is hard to maintain. Must the media's expansion of public space lead to a demand for transparency and widespread immediacy? Or rather, shouldn't we reflect on what absolutely must be public and what can, if only momentarily, remain out of the limelight? The word *secret* unfortunately echoes back to the mysteries of former powers, but there are also temporary secrets, like those that allow seeds to germinate, and nothing says that syndicated or political life must necessarily, at every moment, submit to the law of publicity.

It is said that the *masses* fall easily under the sway of compelling images, whereas the public that reads—or that read—reasons and reflects. But to be moved and to reason, to feel and to judge, are these necessarily contradictory? Should we reason without emotion and without any passion? Metaphysics still comes to haunt our thinking and leads again to simplifying dualities, like that of reason and passion.

The fact of having to reckon with human "passions," circumstantial or recurrent, of knowing that they can be moderated and not destroyed, legitimizes the place that public opinion and rhetoric play in political life. This does not imply any resignation to the irrational but, rather, the integration of passions into political rationality. Rational conduct does not deny human tendencies, or passions; it tries hard to recognize them. Since Freud and Spinoza, we have suspected that there are good passions (like the aspiration for peace or happiness) that can triumph over bad ones and there is no single, pure, reason. This is all the more true because as a calculating power, reason can serve the most sinister ambitions and is no guarantee—we know only too well—against any sort of madness. Also, it will not do to valorize reason (the reason of the elite) over passions (the passions of the people) or to oppose the rationality of discourse to the sentimentality of images. Public opinion combines the two, just as individual judgment does.

In addition, why must intellectual analysis be incompatible with the feelings or the image of adversity with commitment? There has never been commitment without emotion. It is as futile to want to exclude emotions from the city-state as to want to rid discourse of rhetoric. Emotion is not in any way illegitimate. Thus a democracy cannot separate a priori, or by relying on distinguishing the different media, the good public from the bad, and the legitimate opinion from the suspect one.

The Image's Ambiguity

No orator—preacher, politician, lawyer—has been able to function without compelling "images"—in the literary as well as pictorial sense. Previously in the courts, images were used that were painted especially to move the judges. No one is ever enlightened without concrete examples, and "images" in the rhetorical sense, with their illustrative value, had no less effect in the past than visual images have today. The word can even produce a *greater* effect than images, and we no doubt overestimate the impact of modern indexical images, like televised reports.

But if emotion is not to be condemned, it is not necessarily the *screen* that moves and *writing* that instructs. The medium counts as much as the art of using it. The "roughest" images from a news report are often *less* moving than more constructed images from fiction. Of course, even a news report is "fabricated," framed, cut, and mounted, and the "direct" is always a composition. But if a report is neither constructed nor composed so as to offer a narrative framework, the "realistic effect" will be poor, and the emotion, in the end, superficial. Outside any story and without discourse to give it meaning, even the image of a dying child becomes an abstraction: it appalls us more because of the emotion that it does *not* evoke in us, or not enough, than because of the emotion it does. That unknown, even sorrowful face, perceived for an instant after so many others, is not so moving as we claim or would like to believe. Precisely because it is separated from a context and any knowledge that would give it meaning, the filmed or even the photographed face displays an abstract singularity.

To arouse emotion, a legend must be deliberately created. In 1998, the photo of an Algerian woman became in the press the image of a Mater Dolorosa. The *legend* indicated that she had lost her eight children, victims of a massacre. But the legend, fortunately enough, was mistaken, and the woman, whom a journalistic obscenity went so far as to cite among "the ten women of the year," lodged a complaint against the photographer, whose shot had meanwhile won awards. It became apparent that the expected, and perhaps achieved, effect of the photo was linked to the terrible and deceptive legend that tried to make the public believe that an image could make them *see* the pain of a mother whose children have been massacred. Of course, no such thing can be seen. Certain kinds of pain cannot be shown on any face, whether it is seen, photographed, or painted. The ancients, more inspired, considered a painter's best solution to be veiling the face of a father whose daughter was being sacrificed.[1]

Claude Lanzmann's choice for his film *Shoah* was to not allow himself any image that might attempt to show the extermination itself or to provide a visible representation of it, necessarily derisory and false. In this case, the image's powerlessness is not accidental but essential. Nevertheless, certain images are important, even to Lanzmann's film, for example, the images of the tracks at the Sobibor railway station. In filming them, the filmmaker had the witnesses repeat that the tracks were "exactly the same."[2] To get to the crime committed there half a century ago, much more than knowledge or representations is needed. There also must be *traces*, that is, reminders and material marks, objects that have not changed, as if those alone could convince us that we still inhabit the same world and can make the past "reach" us in some way. The documents, the places, the objects, retain an irreplaceable role because they are, in the present world, the remains or the imprints of what has passed.

If Christian painting did not imitate Timanthe's choice and was able to represent a very beautiful Pietà, it is because the image of the Virgin at the death of Christ was not supposed to show the despair of a mother holding her dead son in her arms but the completely reverent sadness of a woman who can overcome her grief through her faith. Mary represents religious love and reconciliation but not the pain of irreparable separation. Her image must make us think of the Resurrection, not death. The artistic problem is not any simpler, of course, but this explains why this image of grief, far from having been veiled, could represent love in such a profound way.

Be that as it may, it would be useless to underestimate the image or to condemn it in general, opposing it to the word. The two always work together.

Truth and Lies

The possibility of the lie does not stem from the use of one particular means, but from a strategy. That is why by nature, the photographic image is neither true or false. It hides what it does not show, of course, just as discourse is silent about what it does not say. But unlike a speaker, an indexical image is taken to be *objective* a priori. Speech is only testimony; the indexical image seems to be proof (despite all the doctoring that can be done to it, especially with new technologies multiplying those possibilities).

This illusion stems from the *realistic effect* of photography. Contrary to representations derived from a drawing—from a *design*, in both senses of the word—which are perceived as fictions, indexical images are the very traces of the things. Thus they seem a priori more "reliable" than discourse.

Nevertheless, a filmed image can deceive as well, or even better, than the words of a witness. The dangers of the fictitious documentary, for example, were assessed long ago. One of the most horribly notorious cases is the film of Nazi propaganda about the Theresien concentration camp: deported Jews had to play their own roles for the camera, pretending to work and to amuse themselves, in order to give the German public the image of a normal and happy social life in a town that was pure propaganda. After the film was shot, the film's director and walk-ons were exterminated in a real concentration camp (Auschwitz, Treblinka, or Sobibor).[3]

Thus the objectivity of indexical images is clearly not enough to guarantee the "truth" of what they show, since they can retain the trace of a "real" scene as well as that of a "simulated" scene. The camera is always innocent: it films or photographs the true or the false equally, the real house by the side of the road or the painted facade of a set behind which there is nothing. The difference between a false documentary showing a fictitious scene and a film of fiction constructed like a true documentary cannot be easily seen. With theater, though, it is a matter of bringing into play the stage as well as the fictional space. No illusion there: the representation presents itself for what it is, and the scenery, even painted in trompe-l'oeil, does not claim to belong to the shared world of the audience.

The suspicion that weighs on indexical images has its own limits, however, because certain images cannot be fictions. Staying with the history of World War II, let us think, for example, of the films that showed the whole world the extermination camps of Nazi Germany: they constituted true proof. It was not that without images, we could not in some way have known of the existence of the camps. Otherwise, you might well say, since there are no photos or films at our disposal, we do not know whether or not the battle of Austerlitz took place! Nor is it a matter of knowing whether the image is capable of showing the thing itself, its essence or its horror—we have just seen that it is not. It is a matter of the impossibility of putting certain images in doubt. Because the emaciated bodies, the frantic eyes, the piles of corpses, cannot have been simulated. No one could produce these death camps except true henchmen. Closer to us in time, the images of the genocide victims in Rwanda or the Kosovo deportees with their long processions of families in tears, old people, and terror-stricken children are not and *cannot* be staged.

That is why henceforth images are part of the means used to establish the facts, and if they do not speak for themselves, they require words. They do not render all "lying" impossible (it never is), but new reporting constitutes, in relation to the word, another source of knowledge and a true opposition force. It prevents ideological discourse and official interpretations from turning in on themselves, which is why authoritarian regimes exercise very strict control over the image, entirely subject to the logic of propaganda. When you want to hide the crime, you forbid the image, you chase away the journalists and photographers. By ensuring their free movement, democracies require themselves to take images into account, even if the "logic of war" limits this freedom—to the extent that we cannot show everything to the enemy.

The Compression of Time

We cannot abstractly define the information techniques or public spaces naturally appropriate to democracy; we can only define the ways of making democracy vital using those means proper to each epoch. The distance between the Third Republic and today's politics is not one that separates a world of reason from a world of feeling, the slow and considered word from the live images created to move us: rather, we find there the emergence of new rhetorics and the superimposition of different techniques with all their virtues and vices.

Nonetheless, the modern media pose specific problems to political and everyday life by imposing their rhythms on our existence. They call into question the usual relationship to duration by continually invalidating one piece of news with the next one. As spectators and in a race for information, journalists seem to work to invalidate time, to systematically reduce all duration rather than taking into account the time that most actions require.

It is a tendency characteristic of all observers in general—and, consequently, belonging as much to the spectator as to the theoretician—to want to judge the results and always to attempt to anticipate the end. We can note this same impatience in the practice of polls. Organizations simulate far-off electoral situations and ask questions that will actually be asked, but differently, some years later.

Why crush time like this? What is it that obliges us to let ourselves be deprived of the true duration of things in this way? The media "time machines" establish us within a kind of impatience that nothing justifies at a time when our destination, near or distant, has become uncertain. Like Benjamin's stroller, our contemporaries dream instead of finally becoming available to time and not of being continually deprived of it.

One of the problems posed by audio or visual images—radio, television, video, photography—is that the public forgets they are constructed. They seem to show reality itself, immediate, "live." Even if it does not function at all like pictorial or theatrical representation, television is still a particular mode of "representation" or "presentation." But on the evening news, it reconstructs only a minute of images and three sentences of discourse from some political event, for example, a party conference. Treated in this way, the news is reduced to a brief survey—a tiny slice of time—that "represents" the event. The public knows that that distance between the reality and its televisual representation is not abolished. Despite that, because of the indexical nature of the images and fascinated by the realistic effect of the news report, we forget the framing, the montaging, *the compression of the time of the event.* With an oral account, we know what it summarizes and what we hope it synthesizes. With the mini-report, we believe that we are witnessing the event, since we have at our disposal simple audio-visual "takes" that must be considered as such.

It is very difficult to escape the reductive effects of images except by exposing media techniques to the public and revealing how images are constructed, as much under ordinary conditions as when they are used tendentiously. This exposure, which cannot be simply theoretical, requires that we analyze the ways of making them. It is toward this healthy examination that a broadcast like *Arrêt sur images* is working.[4] The other means of allowing the public to escape the spell of the image—or of sound—is by teaching children how to use a camera or a microphone themselves. There is no faster way of making the effects of framing, montage, or mixing understood and thus of initiating the public into media "representation." The image is not disqualified in this way, since it is a method of presentation that allows us to see and to think, but we must remember that it reveals only by concealing, as does any (re)presentation.

In addition to the rushing or the compression of time, which especially applies to news broadcasts, there is an economizing of time by the media, the logic of which is not always understood. Also, many people discredit any media expression on the grounds that speaking time is always insufficient. But must the so-called cultural programs be condemned, a few vestiges of which remain on the French channels in those hours reserved for the nonworking population, under the pretext that they allow their participants too little time? To the extent that social time is artificial all the way through, that our use of time is only naturally limited by exhaustion, sleep, and death, speaking time is a convention, and it is not always unreasonable, wherever we are, to "make it brief." Nevertheless, how do you talk about a book or a film, even explain a policy, in a few minutes? The absurdity of that seems obvious and its failure a given. But this reasoning is itself *too brief*, since there is never time a priori suitable for speaking. In many cases, the invasive flood of useless talk or too lengthy writing must be reduced. Not all forms of discourse or exchange necessitate the same level of language or the same amount of time. Furthermore, we are not posing the question of time properly if we suppose that the audiovisual media must compete with or replace other forms of information, culture, or political life. We cannot expect the television—or criticism—to spare audiences the necessity of reading. But knowing how to encourage reading requires a particular kind of rhetoric that, without giving way to slogan, must not replace books themselves. From a democratic perspective, the most serious problem the media pose concerning time is more one of programs and schedules than of the length of an interview. Scheduling the most instructive or the most demanding programs—or simply even subtitled films—at the end of the evening systematically excludes the youngest audience or those who must go to work early in the morning. That includes many, many people, for whom the dullness of "prime time" is too often reserved.

Criticism of the audiovisual media often feeds on nostalgia for writing and for the book. But once we admit that one cannot replace the other, something of which each and everyone of us will easily be convinced, is the opposition between the written and the oral as simple as it seems? The book lost its specific nature as soon as the conditions for producing it allowed for printing texts that were *spoken* as often as truly *written*. Here again, the medium does nothing by itself and offers no guarantee. And speech is not always improvised. Oral discourse on the radio or television is in part precisely written, composed in advance to be spoken. Editorial writers rarely leave their sentences to chance, and radiotelephonic broadcasts are sometimes very carefully composed. Sometimes the *text* is actually written out, word by word, before being read on the air; sometimes after having recorded improvisations or documents, the director composes a broadcast beginning with cutting and montaging, thus practicing true radiotelephonic writing.[5]

Thus even when faced with a media reality that is, for the most part, disappointing, it is more interesting to think about and to work on the use of the media by developing their possibilities than to condemn instruments with democratic potential, often by giving in to the nostalgia for older forms.

Assembled Public, Dispersed Public

The temptation to be nostalgic also exists with regard to political life. Attachment to old techniques—like the idealized assembly of antiquity or the primacy given to writing in the Age of Enlightenment—leaves us looking longingly at two great models: the model of speech before an assembled public and the model of writing before a dispersed public.

It is because of Malesherbes that we have the useful distinction between the two types of public: the assembled public, united physically and in a single place, and the dispersed public, for which the prototype is the reader.[6] Today, radio listeners, television viewers, and electronic communications users also constitute a *dispersed* public. There is no reason to limit the "true public" to an assembled public, as Habermas seems to want to do.[7]

If readers can form a possible model of the public, dispersed listeners and viewers can, too. Discussion, a form of debate that takes place between physically present interlocutors, is only one possible model for public space. This model is not obsolete; it has even been revived by the media, but it does not exhaust the idea of democratic public debate.

Indeed, a limited conception of debate leads Habermas to discredit media communication, which he labels "unilateral" and manipulative. This disqualification, no doubt derived from totalitarian examples, depends on a conception of the public taken up by C. Wright Mills and according to which in a public—as opposed to the "masses"—"there are at least as many individuals who express an opinion as individuals who receive it." Moreover, "an effective and immediate response to any opinion expressed"[8] must be authorized, which is not the case for the public of the media. But we might wonder for what public such immediacy would be possible! In any case, a single response is not "immediately" possible, even in a small gathering. No group, no assembly, by the sole fact that it is a multiplicity, permits everyone to respond, much less to respond immediately or to have access to the *same speaking time*. Any public debate, in fact, implies waiting periods, time lags, delays between speeches and responses. A discussion with many involves procedures, mediation, protocol, and even hierarchies. For each interlocutor, the moment when he can speak and the length of his remarks are the object of complex, sometimes invisible, rules, as much in a democratic assembly as elsewhere—on the television set or in the classroom. The very weight of a speaker's words depends largely on his status or authority, which no egalitarian principle can erase or impose. By multiplying the voices and compelling them to listen to one another, a debate, even within an assembled public, is always a way of giving time to communication but also of *temporizing* the exchange and *forcing each individual to wait*. Public debate must not be turned into a frustrating trial for the sake of the immediacy of exchanges. The idea that a "true public," in the sense of an assembled public, allows for the immediate reciprocity of exchanges becomes a myth as soon as we go beyond a very small number of individuals, let us say three or four, and, consequently, as soon as it is a matter of a public. In other words, if discussion is *always* more or less spaced and temporized, it does not essentially suffer from the distance between interlocutors or the intervals between exchanges, and the debate can take place just as well within a dispersed public.

That the reciprocity not be *without delay*, through writing or over the air waves, does not, in effect, prohibit or weaken the public nature of an argument. Of course, the television viewer (or listener) does not respond directly to the orator to whom he listens, but neither does the reader respond to the author whose works he is reading—and he is no less part of a public worthy of that name. What gives an opinion its public nature is, first of all, its visibility. It is in thinking of this criterion that Gabriel Tarde was able to say of modern publics that they were more *audiences* than assemblies conceived according to the ancient model.[9] But publicity itself is not enough to establish a *democratic* debate if those who express themselves, whatever the distance, do not listen to or respond to one another. In this respect, and should there be a desire to contest the appropriation of public opinion by a small number of voices or signatures, it would be necessary to extend the *right to respond* much more widely, a right little exercised or respected in fact by either the press or the audiovisual media. Thus the criterion of democratic debate is that the participants listen to or read to one another and not that they be physically assembled.

In this sense, electronic communication could satisfy the conditions for a public scene. By right, if not in fact, everyone can be connected to everyone else, and these are favorable conditions for discussion. However, electronic communication space is divided into such a great number of different sites that communications there are often private exchanges more than public discussions. Nevertheless, today, electronic connections allow important networks to be formed. We can see virtual communities developing in which public opinion takes shape (and whose members can decide to come together physically). Thus the computer is giving rise to new public scenes.

In another way, the media public is dispersed differently from readers or Internet users. Listeners and viewers can witness, for example, *simultaneously* and in great numbers, a demonstration, a live news report, a debate; they can even watch a sit-com at the same time. Spatially dispersed, the media public is *temporally* united and can think of itself as a theater audience that witnesses "together," that is, simultaneously, the same show (moreover, theatergoers sit next to each other but do not talk to each other). To be part of a single public is already to share the same world, to belong to one and the same "community." In general, we like to know what others know and see what others see, and it is just as much on shared references—realities and fictions—as it is on collective rhythms that the shared world is constructed.

Close-ups

Therefore the instruments of our time lead less to a loss or a diminishment of old forms of political life—because how were the people informed in the past; what were their means of thinking, debating, deciding?—than to a reframing of the common space. A strange reframing, no doubt, that lays out virtual scenes where the dispersed public contemplates terribly real cathodic phantoms, but without these, could the many peoples of today's democracies still picture their identity?

The screen always hides at the same time as it shows; it simultaneously distances and brings closer. Is democracy lost that way as much as is feared? However much the beings populating the screen are seen from a distance, they also are familiar and infinitely closer than the orators of long ago, whom the people knew only through the newspapers.

Paradoxically—although this is a paradox with which we are familiar today—the media image creates a great proximity with public figures. This is not at all an illusion of proximity; it is a true closeness. The look, the voice, the attitude, and the style of a man or woman are not only perceivable but enlarged by the image, and we know someone better, even if unilaterally, by seeing him often on television than by encountering him from a distance at public gatherings. The proximity by image has become so routine that it is being introduced into conferences and large meetings by cameras and screens that function in-house, as if it was no longer tolerable to see someone *from a distance*. Henceforth we need "close-ups," representations that draw near.

But if the media have become an inescapable public space, they do not replace intermediary organizations (places of work, struggle, clubs, associations, parties, and the like), that is, internal democratic scenes without which society is fragmented. Thus it is a question of knowing whether it is possible to regulate the interfaces between the different spaces better, so as to maintain communication between them, notably between the small public assemblies and the dispersed publics, and to make it so that media time does not destroy other forms of encounters.

The People Embodied

Nevertheless, how can we not recognize that the public space of screens lacks live bodies? Politics cannot find its only place there any more than speech can be its only element.

Politics will never be limited to questions of communication and discussion because the political community—and, first of all, society itself—is made up of flesh-and-blood human beings. It is a physical community that, even while identifying itself with verbal or symbolic expression, cannot be reduced to that. Discourse is not everything.

Virtual communications and disembodied Internet associations exist, reduced on the screen to a symbolic existence, but in front of those screens, there are living beings. These are the ones who make up society, with their needs, their joys and suffering, their hopes and their fears. We can computerize administration, but we cannot computerize politics because the city-state is composed of flesh-and-blood beings. In the necessity to feed and shelter and care for ourselves, to live, to leave a habitable world for our descendants, there resides the economic body. In the desire to live well and in freedom resides the political body.

Thus political life unites living beings who, when they deem necessary, never fail to remind the ruling power that they are, in the final analysis, physical forces and not just a public opinion and voters. Street demonstrations are as much demonstrations of power as means of expression. However much the confrontation between the people's and the state's power is regulated by a political and legal organization, it will never be obliterated or disappear. Beneath the most democratic institutions, behind the discourse and the images, the physical existence of the people survives. Reasonable *and* impassioned, full of patience *and* impatience, it remains the horizon and the limit of all representation.

But how do modern peoples experience their relationship to time? Such a question would demand a new approach. It would be necessary to know how to define a people without gods anymore and without faith in the promises of history. Such a people, like each human generation, would discover its finitude; it would assume the contingency and the discontinuity of its history and would not let itself be trapped in either nostalgia for origins or a law of forever-deferred fulfillment. Nevertheless, by very reason of its new relationship to time, this modern people could still affirm the value of the passing and the lasting, that is, the meaning of what, beyond the death of individuals, deserves to survive.

Notes

. . . . .

THE WESTERN HOUR

1. See especially Georg Wilhelm Friedrich Hegel, *La Raison dans l'histoire* (Paris: Plon, "10–18" collection, 1965), p. 280.

2. Georg Wilhelm Friedrich Hegel, *Phénoménologie de l'esprit* (Paris: Aubier, 1947), preface, p. 12.

3. Hegel, *La Raison dans l'histoire*, p. 48.

4. Krzysztof Pomian, *L'Ordre du temps* (Paris: Gallimard, 1984).

5. See the essay by Jacques Le Goff, "Au Moyen Âge, temps de l'église et temps du marchand," in *Pour un autre Moyen Âge* (Paris: Gallimard, 1977), pp. 46 ff. Republished in the "Quarto" collection, 1999.

6. See Marc Augé's *Pour une anthropologie des mondes contemporains* (Paris: Aubier, "Critiques" collection, 1994).

7. Ibid.

PASSAGE

1. See Theodor W. Adorno, *Sur Walter Benjamin* (Paris: Allia, 1999), p. 37; and Walter Benjamin, *Sens unique* preceded by *Enfance berlinoise* (Paris: Les Lettres nouvelles–Maurice Nadeau, 1978).

2. See François Hartog, "Time, History and the Writing of History: The Order of Time," in *History-Making: The Intellectual and Social Formation of a Discipline*, ed. R. Torstendahl (Stockholm, 1996), pp. 95–113. For Hartog, the regime of modern historicity corresponds to the teleological conception of history. He opposes it to an older regime of historicity, according to which the present is illuminated by the light of the past, not the future. Also see the volume entitled *Actualités du contemporain*, particularly Jacques Revel's "Pratiques du contemporain et régimes d'historicité," *Le Genre humain*, no. 35 (Paris: Éditions du Seuil, 2000).

3. Johann Wolfgang von Goethe, *Faust*, lines 12.104 and 12.105. The adjective *vergänglich* means "passing," "transitory." *Das Vergängliche* is the corresponding noun and can be translated as "the passing" or "the ephemeral." *Das Vergänglichkeit* names, in a comprehensive fashion, the ephemeral nature of things. This is the title Freud gave to an article written in 1915, translated as "Ephémère destinée," in *Résultats, idées, problèmes*, 1, 1890–1920 (Paris: PUF, "Bibliothèque de psychanalyse," 1988), pp. 233–236. *Vergänglichkeit* has also been translated as the neologism "passagèreté" ("passingness"), a word that ordinarily designates the migration of certain birds and that I have adopted here.

4. Freud, "Ephémère destinée," p. 234.

5. I have already outlined an apology for oblivion in "Le prix de l'oubli," ch. 1 of my *Volume. Philosophies et politiques de l'architecture* (Paris: Galilée, 1992), in reference to *Cinq leçons sur la psychanalyse* (Paris: Payot, 1973). There Freud describes hysterical symptoms as commemorative symbols and proposes that hysterics "do not free themselves from the past and ignore the reality of the present."

6. All change, wrote Aristotle, "is by nature unmaking"—"*Metbolè pāsa phúsei ekstatikón*" (Physics, IV, 13, 222b 16). Pierre Aubenque insists on the double meaning of *ekstatikón*, which evokes the phenomenon of leaving the self, of plunging into ecstasy. The being is put "out of the self" by movement. This ecstasy "is manifested in the rhythmic structure of time." It is the source of aging and wear but also of becoming and fulfillment. See Pierre Aubenque, *Le Problèm de l'être chez Aristotle* (Paris: PUF, 1966), p. 433.

7. Socrates, *Phaedo*, 83, 84.

8. Martin Heidegger, *Les Concepts fondamentaux de la métaphysique: Monde, finitude, solitude*, trans. Daniel Panis (Paris: Gallimard, 1992), p. 21 (1929–1930 course).

9. Ibid.

10. See the chapter "Historical Polemic" in this book.

11. Michel Montaigne, *Les Essais*, book 3, ch. 2: "Du repentir."

12. Maurice Merleau-Ponty, *Éloge de la philosophie* (1953) (Paris: Gallimard, "Idées" collection, 1985), p. 72.

13. Catherine Malabou, *L'Avenir de Hegel: Plasticité, temporalité, dialectique* (Paris: Vrin, 1996), p. 166.

14. Michel Foucault, *Les Mots et les choses* (Paris: Gallimard, 1966), pp. 328–29.

15. Jean-Luc Nancy, *Hegel: L'Inquiétude du négatif* (Paris: Hachette, 1997), p. 40.

16. According to the prelude to Hesiod's *Theogeny*: "Before all was Abyss; then Earth with the wide flanks, solidly seated to be forever offered to all the living," trans. Paul Mazon (Paris: Les Belles Lettres, 1960).

17. Jean-Pierre Vernant, *L'Univers, les dieux, les hommes: Récits grecs des origines* (Paris: Éditions du Seuil, "La Librairie du XXe siècle," 1999), p. 22.

THE RETREAT OF THE ETERNAL

1. Along with Pierre Aubenque, we can consider movement to be what allows us to define, according to Aristotle, what belongs to the sublunar world, whereas the divine is immutable. The circular movement of the stars does not constitute an objection to this principle of division because its cyclical nature, purely repetitive, aligns it with immobility. See Pierre Aubenque, *Le Problème de l'être chez Aristotle* (Paris: PUF, 1966), pp. 412 ff., and p. 418, n. 2.

2. See Plato, *Parmenides*, 123, d, 1–4.

3. See, for example, Friedrich Wilhelm Nietzsche, *The Anti-Christ*, sec. 6.

4. For Aristotle, "form" does not involve the appearance of things but, rather, their essence. The term comes from the Latin *forma*, which is the translation of the Greek *eïdos*, *morphè*, and *ousía*.

5. On the paradoxical status of the feminine in generation, see Sylviane Agacinski, "Le Tout premier écart," in *Les Fins de l'homme: À partir du travail de Jacques Derrida* (Cerisy conference) (Paris: Galilée, 1985).

6. Aristotle, *Ethics*, II, 3.

7. Aristotle, *Metaphysics*, Δ 30.

MOVEMENT

1. Aristotle, *Physics*, IV, 219a.

2. See Maurice Merleau-Ponty, *Phénoménologie de la perception* (1945) (Paris: Gallimard, 1964), p. 492.

3. See the first part of Immanuel Kant, "L'Esthétique transcendantale," sec. 4, in *Critique de la raison pure* (Paris: PUF, 1965), p. 61.

4. Ibid., sec. 2, p. 55.

5. Ibid., p. 56.

6. Ibid., sec. 4, p. 61.

7. Roger Verneaux, *Vocabulaire de Kant* (Paris: Aubier-Montaigne, 1967), p. 105.

8. Saint Augustine, *The Confessions*, ch. 26.

9. Translation by H. Dussort (Paris: PUF, 1964).

10. See Maurice Merleau-Ponty, "La temporalité," part 3, ch. 2, of *Phénoménologie de la perception* (1945) (Paris: Gallimard, 1964); Jacques Derrida, *Le Problème de la genèse dans la philosophie de Husserl* (Paris: PUF, 1990).

11. Aristotle, *Physics*, IV, 220b.

12. According to Einstein's theory of relativity, for one observer, two events can take place simultaneously, but for another observer, they do not.

13. That is, the sky, the sphere on which the stars seem fixed.

14. See Krzysztof Pomian, *L'Ordre du temps* (Paris: Gallimard, 1984).

15. Aristotle, *Physics*, IV, 223b.

16. See I. Progogine, *La Fin des certitudes* (Paris: Odile Jacob, 1996).

17. See Aristotle, *La Poétique*, trans. R. Dupont-Roc and J. Lallot (Paris: Éditions du Seuil, 1980), ch. 6, pp. 53–55; and Paul Ricoeur, *L'Intrigue et le récit historique* (1983), vol. 1 of *Temps et récit* (Paris: Éditions du Seuil, "Points Essais" collection, 1991), pp. 66 ff.

18. Jean-Pierre Vernant, *Chronos, pour l'intelligence du partage temporel* (Paris: Grasset, "Le collège de philosophie" collection, 1997), p. 107.

UN PASSEUR DE TEMPS: WALTER BENJAMIN

1. Walter Benjamin, *Das Passagen-Werk* (Frankfurt am Main: Suhrkamp Ver-

lag, 1982); and *Paris: Capitale du XIXe siècle. Le Livres des passages*, trans. from German by Jean Lacoste (Paris: Éditions de Cerf, 1989), p. 435.

2. Philippe-Alain Michaud, *Aby Warburg et l'image en mouvement*, preface by Georges Didi-Huberman (Paris: Macula, 1998), p. 177. On Aby Warburg, see the chapter "Anarchronisms of Art" in this book.

3. Georges Bataille, *L'Expérience intérieure* (1943) (Paris: Gallimard, "Tel" collection, 1979), p. 39.

4. I am thinking especially of Michel de Certeau and Arlette Farge.

5. Benjamin, *Le Livre des passages*, p. 434.

6. Ibid., p. 132.

7. Julian Gracq drew inspiration from this phrase for the title of his book on Nantes: *La Forme d'une ville* (Paris: José Corti, 1985).

8. Benjamin, *Le Livre des passages*, p. 870.

9. Aloïs Riegl, *Le Culte moderne des monuments: Son essence et sa genèse* (1903) (Paris: Éditions du Seuil, 1984).

10. Paul Valéry, "Le Bilan de l'intelligence" (1935), in *Oeuvres complètes* (Paris: Gallimard, "Bibliotheque de la Pléiade" collection), vol. 1, p. 1063.

HISTORICAL POLEMIC

1. This kind of history also involves nature—contrary to the classical conception of a nature that repeats itself—when, for example, the stars start to produce more and more atoms or when a landslide or a volcanic eruption occurs on the surface of our planet.
An earlier version of these pages, "Modernités esthétiques," appeared in the journal *Rue Descartes*, no. 10 (Paris: Albin Michel, 1994).

2. Pierre Aubenque, *Le Problèm de l'être chez Aristotle* (Paris: PUF, 1966), p. 491.

3. Aristotle, *Nicomachean Ethics*, I, 7, 17.

4. André Leroi-Gourhan, *Le Geste et la parole: La Mémoire et les rythmes* (Paris: Albin Michel, 1964), vol. 2, p. 50 (italics added).

5. Ibid.

6. Quatremère de Quincy, *De l'imitation* (Brussels, AAM Editions, 1980).

7. Charles-Pierre Baudelaire, *Le Peintre de la vie moderne*, in *Ecrits esthétiques* (Paris: Union générale d'édition, "10–18" collection, 1986), ch. 4, "La Modernité," p. 372.

8. Baudelaire, "Le Public moderne et la photographie," Salon 1859, in *Ecrits esthétiques*, p. 290.

9. Ibid., p. 287.

10. Baudelaire, "La Modernité," in *Le Peintre de la vie moderne*, in *Ecrits esthétiques*, p. 373.

11. Ibid., p. 375.

12. Baudelaire, "Le Public moderne et la photographie," p. 289.

13. Baudelaire calls him M.G.: "I want to talk about the drawing method of M.G."; see *Le Peintre de la vie moderne*, ch. 5, "L'Art mnémonique," p. 376.

14. "De la connaissance des arts fondés sur le Dessin, et particulièrement de la peinture, par M.C*****," in *Mercure de France* 1 (March 1759): 177.

15. Baudelaire, "L'Art mnémonique," p. 376.

16. See Erwin Panofsky, *Idea: Contribution à l'histoire du concept de l'ancienne théorie de l'art* (Paris: Gallimard, "Idées" collection, 1983), ch. 4.

17. Unless otherwise indicated, the quotations from Baudelaire are from "L'Art mnémonique," in *Le Peintre de la vie moderne*.

18. Quatremère de Quincy emphasizes that "the various imitative arts are not human inventions, fanciful creations that can be extended or modified at will." According to him, as a particular type of imitation, each art has its own processes, objects, and effects, which it cannot borrow from others (*De l'imitation*, part 1, par. 3). Note that this work, from 1823, is contemporaneous with the very first images of Nicéphore Niepce.

19. Baudelaire, "Le Public moderne et la photographie," p. 290.

20. I borrow Delacroix's expressions here as quoted by V. Kahnen in *La Photographie est-elle un art?* trans. A. Frejer (Paris: Le Chêne, 1974), p. 14.

21. On all this modern spiritualism in Russia, see Jean-Claude Marcadé, "L'Obsession du spirituel dans l'avant-garde russe, avant et après la révolution de 1917," in *Qu'est-ce que l'art au XXe siècle?* (Paris: Éditions de l'École nationale des beaux-Arts). Marcadé quotes Kandinsky in a very illuminating way: "There could not be perfect form without perfect content: spirit determines matter, and not the other way around. . . . The great broom of history that will clean up the filth of exteriority[;] the interior spirit will appear here also as the final impartial judge." Also see Dimitri Merejkovski, *Un nouveau pas vers l'avènement du mufleroi* (1914): "Futurism is not the af-

firmation of the mechanical but of 'machismo,' in other words, the affirmation of the lack of soul. . . . Futurism is the song of the slaves of the machine, which has sovereignty over the world." In French, see Kasimir Malévitch, *Le Miroir suprématiste* (Lausanne: L'Âge d'homme, 1977), p. 147.

22. Michel Henry, "Réinventer la culture," *Le Monde des débats*, no. 11 (September 1993); and *La Barbarie* (Paris: Grasset, 1987).

23. See Michel Henry, *Voir l'invisible* (Paris: François Bourin, 1988), p. 74.

24. Quatremère de Quincy, *De l'imitation* (Brussels, AAM Editions, 1980).

25. See Quatremère de Quincy, "Copier," in *Dictionnaire de l'architecture* de Quatremère de Quincy and also in *De l'imitation*, p. 50.

26. Walter Benjamin, *L'Oeuvre d'art à l'époque de sa reproduction mécanisée*, republished in *Ecrits français*, introduction by Jean-Maurice Monnoyer (Paris: Gallimard, "Bibliothèque des idées" collection, 1991).

27. On the specific nature of the photographic image as an imprint (or indexical image), see Roland Barthes, *La Chambre claire* (Paris: Gallimard, 1989); Jean-Marie Shaeffer, *L'Image précaire: Du dispositif photographique* (Paris: Éditions du Seuil, 1987); Rosalind Kraus, *Le Photographique: Pour une théorie des écarts*, preface by Hubert Damisch (Paris: Macula, 1991); as well as the several works by Georges Didi-Huberman cited here.

28. Benjamin, *L'Oeuvre d'art à l'époque de sa reproduction mécanisée*, in *Ecrits français*, p. 142 (italics in original).

29. See C. S. Peirce, *Écrits sur le signe* (Paris: Éditions du Seuil, 1978), pp. 153–56.

30. Barthes, *La Chambre claire*, p. 127.

31. It is the *punctum* in it that "pierces me" (Barthes, *La Chambre claire*, p. 49).

THE EPOCH OF PHANTOMS

1. On the symbolic value of the photographic act, see Serge Tisseron, *Le Mystère de la chambre claire* (Paris: Flammarion, 1996).

2. See the analysis by Pierre Bourdieu in *Un art moyen*, ed. Pierre Bourdieu (Paris: Éditions de Minuit, 1965.

3. See the chapter "Historical Polemic" in this book.

4. On the invention of chronophotography, see Michel Frizot, *Étienne-Jules Marey* (Paris: National Center of Photography, "Photo poche" collection, 1984).

5. Like Zuccari or Lomazzo. See Erwin Panofsky, *Idea: Contribution à l'histoire du concept de l'ancienne théorie de l'art* (Paris: Gallimard, "Idées" collection, 1983), ch. 4.

6. See Charles-Pierre Baudelaire, *Le Peintre de la vie moderne*, in *Ecrits esthétiques* (Paris: Union générale d'édition, "10–18" collection, 1986), ch. 5, "L'Art mnémonique"; and the chapter "Historical Polemic" in this book.

7. Gotthold E. Ephraim Lessing, *Laocoon ou des frontières de la peinture et de la poésie* (1766) (Paris: Hermann, 1990), p. 56.

8. Louis Marin, *De la représentation* (Paris: Gallimard–Éditions du Seuil, "Hautes études" collection, 1994), ch. 17, "Déposition du temps dans la représentation peinte," p. 282 ff.

9. See Sören Kierkegaard, *Fear and* Trembling, 15th ed., trans. Alastair Hannay (New York: Viking-Penguin, 1986). On Abraham's doubt, see Sylviane Agacinski, *Critique de l'égocentrisme: L'Événement de l'autre* (Paris: Galilée, 1996), pp. 111–16.

10. See Immanuel Kant, *Critique de la raison pure*, part 1, book 2, "Du schématisme des concepts purs de l'entendement" (Paris: PUF, 1965), p. 151.

11. Ibid., pp. 152–53 (italics added).

12. Martin Heidegger, *Kant et le problème de la métaphysique*, trans. Alphonse de Waelhens and Walter Beimel (Paris: Gallimard, 1963), p. 153.

13. Ibid., p. 152.

14. Paul Valéry, *Léonard et les philosophes*, in *Oeuvres complètes* (Paris: Gallimard, "Bibliothèque de la Pléiade"), vol. 1, p. 1266 (italics added).

15. Marcel Proust, *À la recherche du temps perdu* (Paris: Gallimard, "Bibliothèque de la Pléiade" collection), vol. 3, p. 886.

16. Georges Didi-Huberman, "Ouverture sur un point de vue anachronique," in *L'Empreinte* (Paris: Georges-Pompidou Center, 1997), p. 19.

17. Pliny the Elder, *Natural History*, vol. 35, ch. 15. Pliny's expression is explained and commented on by Edouard Pommier in *Théories du portrait: De la Renaissance aux Lumières* (Paris: Gallimard, 1998), p. 18.

18. See Régis Debray, "Le Tombeau vide et après," in *L'Oeil naïf* (Paris: Éditions du Seuil, 1994), p. 177.

19. See *Abécédaire de Gilles Deleuze avec Claire Parnet* (video), Éditions Montparnasse, 1997.

20. Film by Woody Allen (1985).

ANACHRONISMS OF ART

1. This is the term used in the definition in the *Petit Robert* (1993).

2. Pierre Francastel, *Art et technique aux XIXe et XXe siècles* (1956) (Paris: Gallimard, "Tel" collection, 1988). Also see Pierre Francastel, *La Figure et le lieu: L'Ordre visuel du quattrocento* (Paris: Gallimard, 1967).

3. Francastel, *Art et technique*, p. 8: "Any idea of progress is absent from such a point of view."

4. Nicole Loraux, "Éloge de l'anachronisme," in *L'Ancien et le nouveau, le henre humain*, no. 27 (Paris: Éditions de Seuil, 1993), pp. 23 ff.

5. See, in particular, Georges Didi-Huberman, "Viscosités et survivances, l'histoire de l'art à l'épreuve de matériau," *Critique*, no. 611 (April 1998) (on the book by Julius von Schlosser, *Histoire du portrait de cire* [1911], trans. E. Pommier [Paris: Macula, 1997]).

6. Von Schlosser, *Histoire du portrait de cire*.

7. "Revenance d'une forme," ch. 5 of *Phasmes* (Paris: Éditions de Minuit, 1998), p. 41.

8. Aby Warburg, *Essais florentins* (Paris: Klincksieck, 1990).

9. E. B. Tylor, *Researches into the Early History of Mankind and the Development of Civilization* (London: Murray, 1865).

10. Letter to Fliess, December 6, 1896, in Sigmund Freud, *La Naissance de la psychanalyse: Lettres à Wilhelm Fliess, notes et plans (1887–1902)*, ed. Marie Bonaparte, Anna Freud, and Ernst Kris; and trans. Anne Berman (Paris: PUF, 1956), pp. 155–56.

11. Leon Battista Alberti, *De Pictura*, book 2 (Paris: Macula-Dédale, 1992).

12. Ibid., p. 131.

13. Aby Warburg, *Images from the Region of the Pueblos Indians of North America* (Ithaca, N.Y.: Cornell University Press, 1995); and Warburg, *Essais florentins*.

14. Warburg, *Images from the Region of the Pueblos Indians*, p. 20.

15. Warburg, *Essais florentins*, p. 126.

16. In the fifteenth century, for example. See Warburg, *Essais florentins*, p. 165.

17. "This will kill that" is the title of a chapter in *Notre-Dame de Paris*, in which Victor Hugo develops the idea that thanks to printing, the book of paper will kill the book of stone, architecture.

18. Warburg, *Essais florentins*, p. 126.

19. Ernst H. Gombrich, *L'Art et l'illusion* (1960), trans. G. Durand (Paris: Gallimard, 1996), p. 75.

20. Warburg, *Essais florentins*, p. 106.

21. Philippe-Alain Michaud, *Aby Warburg et l'image en mouvement*, preface by Georges Didi-Huberman (Paris: Macula, 1998), p. 93.

22. Georges Salles, *Le Regard* (Paris: Plon, 1939), pp. 123–24, quoted by Walter Benjamin in *Écrits français*, p. 328.

23. André Malraux, *Le Musée imaginaire* (1947, rev. ed. 1965) (Paris: Gallimard, "Folio" collection, 1996), p. 256.

24. See the chapter "Historical Polemic" in this book.

25. Published in Benjamin, *Ecrits français*; and see the chapter "Historical Polemic" in this book.

26. Pierre Francastel, *Peinture et society* (Paris: Denoël, 1977), pp. 322–23, n. 77.

27. Ibid.

28. Ibid., p. 158 (italics added).

29. See Vitruvius, *Les Dix Livres d'architecture*, trans. Claude Perrault (1673), revised by A. Dalmas (Paris: Balland, 1979), book 4, ch. 2, p. 127.

30. See Frank Lloyd Wright, *L'Avenir de l'architecture* (Paris: Denoël-Gonthier, "Médiations" collection, 1982), vol. 1, p. 68.

31. Siegfried Gidion, *Espace, temps, architecture* (1940) (Paris: Denoël, 1990), p. 139.

32. The letter of protest, published in *Le Temps*, February 14, 1887, was signed by great names: Guy de Maupassant, Alexandre Dumas, Coppée, Leconte de Lisle, Sully Prudhomme, Charles Gounod, and Charles Garnier, among others.

33. On this controversy, see Bertrand Lemoine, *La Tour de Monsieur Eiffel* (Paris: Gallimard, "Decouvertes" collection, 1989), pp. 98 ff.

34. Quoted by Gidion, *Espace, temps, architecture*, p. 143.

35. See Gilbert Simondon, *Du mode d'existence des objets techniques* (Paris: Aubier, 1958). On the thinking about technology, also see Bernard Stiegler, *La Technique et le temps* (2 vols.) (Paris: Galilée, 1994 and 1996).

36. On the concepts of *fixation*, *viscosity*, and *plasticity of the libido*, see Jean Laplanche and Jean-Bertrand Pontalis, *Vocabulaire de la phychanalyse* (Paris: PUF, 1967).

37. In her thesis *L'Avenir de Hegel* (Paris: Vrin, 1996). The work on plasticity leads Catherine Malabou to suggest here a new reading of the dialectic and temporality in Hegel.

38. Gombrich, *L'Art et l'illusion*, p. 62.

39. An expression of Millet's, quoted by Julia Cartwright in *Jean-François Millet* (London, 1896), p. 161.

40. See Quentin Bajac (director of the Musée d'Orsay exhibit), *Tableaux vivants: Fantaisies photographiques victoriennes (1840–1880)* (Paris: National Museums Conference, 1999).

41. France, we know, also had its pictorialists, like Robert Demachy or Paul Périer, but they did not necessarily create *tableaux vivants*. They attempted above all to soften the plate's precision as much as possible to obtain the appearance of a painted image.

42. Bajac, *Tableaux vivants*, p. 36.

43. Quoted by Bajac, *Tableaux vivants*, p. 20. Thomas Sutton was a member of the Royal Photographic Society, and he had initially defended the idea of the art photography.

44. Vicenzo Danti, *Il primo libro del trattato* (Florence, 1567), quoted by Edouard Pommier, *Théorie du portrait, de la Renaissance aux Lumières* (Paris: Gallimard, "Bibliothèque illustrée des histoires" collection, 1998), p. 141.

45. In Quatremère de Quincy, *De l'imitation* (Brussels, AAM Editions, 1980).

46. Alain Cavalier's superb film *Thérèse* (1986) illustrates, through fiction, the invisibility of saintliness by making the difference between saintliness and neurosis totally indecipherable for the viewer.

47. Letter from David Octavius Hill to Lady Ruthven, December 1847 (quoted in Bajac, *Tableaux vivants*, p. 19). Unlike Sutton, Hill seems to believe in the transformation of bedclothes.

48. Roland Barthes, *La Chambre claire* (Paris: Gallimard, 1989), p. 139 (italics added).

49. X-ray photography, ultrasound, and so forth, have produced images of phenomena inaccessible to our perception until now. In this way, modern imagery has considerably enlarged the field of our potential experience.

50. Like Hill and Adamson.

51. Charles-Pierre Baudelaire, "Le Public moderne et la photographie," in *Écrits esthétiques* (Paris: Union générale d'édition, "10–18" collection, 1986), p.

289. Note that in Paris or for Baudelaire, dressing up is a vulgar pastime for the lower classes and not an aristocratic diversion, as it is for the English.

52. Baudelaire, "Le Public moderne et la photographie," p. 291.

53. *L'Art du nu au XIXe siècle: Le Photographe et son modèle* (catalog of the exhibition at the National Library of France (Paris: Hazan/Bibliothèque nationale de France, October–January 1998).

54. Eugène Delacroix, *Journal*, October 5, 1855 (Paris: Plon, 1893), vol. 3.

55. Quoted in *L'Art du nu au XIXe siècle*, p. 46.

56. A confusion that Benjamin does not always avoid; see the chapter "Historical Polemic" in this book.

57. Antonia Soulez, ed., *Dictées de Wittgenstein à Waismann et pour Schlick* (Paris: PUF, 1997), p. 160.

58. But in *Kant and the Problem of Metaphysics*, Heidegger uses the same word (*Bild*) to refer to both the *view* of a thing and its *image* (see also the chapter "The Epoch of Phantoms" in this book).

59. Soulez, ed., *Dictées de Wittgenstein à Waismann et pour Schlick*, p. 165.

60. Anonymous, *Modèle italian* (1900), in *L'Art du nu au XIXe siècle*, p. 55.

PATIENCE AND DEMOCRACY

1. Jürgen Habermas, *L'Espace public: Archéologie de la publicité comme dimension constructive de la société bourgeoise* (1962) (Paris: Payot, 1986).

2. Régis Debray, *L'État séducteur: Les Révolutions médiologiques du pouvoir* (Paris: Gallimard, 1993).

3. Régis Debray, *Cours de médiologie générale* (Paris: Gallimard, 1991), p. 67.

4. Thomas Hobbes, *Leviathan* (1651).

5. In the classical period, *actor* still designated the character, not the player.

6. See Pierre Rosanvallon, *Le Peuple introuvable: Histoire de la représentation démocratique en France* (Paris: Gallimard, 1998).

7. Habermas, *L'Espace public*.

8. Arlette Farge, *Dire et mal dire: L'Opinion publique au XVIIIe siècle* (Paris: Éditions du Seuil, "La Librairie du XXe siècle," 1992), p. 161.

9. Immanuel Kant, *Qu'est-ce que les Lumières?* (Paris: Flammarion, "GF" collection, 1991).

10. From 1790, Immanuel Kant, *Critique of Judgment*. I am commenting here on sec. 40. Also see sec. 19 to 22.

11. Hannah Arendt, *La Crise de la culture* (*Between Past and Future*, 1954) (Paris: Gallimard, "Idées" collection, 1972), ch. 6, p. 283.

12. Ibid., p. 308.

13. Maurice Merleau-Ponty, *Éloge de la philosophie* (1953) (Paris: Gallimard, "Idées" collection, 1985), pp. 38–40.

14. Ibid. (italics added).

15. Ibid., p. 72.

16. Jean-François Lyotard posed this modern question: how can we presume to judge without criteria, without categories? See *Au juste* (interviews with Jean-Loup Thébaud) (Paris: Christian Bourgois, 1979). Subsequently, Lyotard preferred to label *postmodern* the condition that requires us to judge without knowledge, without rules (*Moralités postmodernes*) (Paris: Galilée, 1993). This problem of judgment makes him turn back again to Kant as well.

17. I am referring here to Jean-Pierre Vernant, *Les Origines de la pensée grecque* (1962) (Paris: PUF, 1983), ch. 3.

18. See Barbara Cassin, *L'Effet sophistique* (Paris: Gallimard, "NRF Essais" collection, 1995), p. 245.

19. Georg Wilhelm Friedrich Hegel, *Principes de la philosophie du droit* (Paris: Gallimard, 1949), sec. 309. But the question here is not one of democracy. The assembly plays a mediating role between the people and the state itself.

20. Guy Debord, *La Société du spectacle* (Paris: Gallimard, "Folio" collection, 1992).

21. Ibid., sec. 20 (italics added).

22. Arendt, "Vérité et politique," in *La Crise de la culture*, p. 314.

MEDIA TIME

1. This pictorial solution is attributed to Timanthe, an Athenian painter from the third century B.C., who had to paint a *Sacrifice of Iphigenia*. Gotthold E. Ephraim Lessing also discusses the reasons for this choice in *Laocoon ou des frontières de la peinture et de la poésie* (1766) (Paris: Hermann, 1990), not seeing it as a weakness of the painting but, rather, as the painter's refusal to show anything ugly, according to classical criteria.

2. See Claude Lanzmann, *Au sujet de "Shoah": Le Film de Claude Lanzmann* (Paris: Belin, 1990), p. 290.

3. On the Therensienstadt ghetto, see, most recently, Claude Lanzmann, *Un vivant qui passe: Auschwitz 1943–Theresien 1944* (Paris: Arte éditions / Mille et une nuits, 1997); Sabine Zeitoun and Dominique Foucher, eds., *Le Masque de la barbarie: Le Ghetto de Therensienstadt 1941–1945* (Lyons, Éditions de la ville de Lyons–Centre d'histoire de la résistance et de la déportation, 1998).

4. By Daniel Schneidermann. Also see, by the same author, an interesting book with the unfortunate title *Du journalisme après Bourdieu* (Paris: Fayard, 1999).

5. I am thinking here especially of *France Culture*.

6. I find this distinction in Roger Chartier, who uses it in his book *Les Origines culturelles de la Révolution française* (Paris: Éditions de Seuil, 1990).

7. Jürgen Habermas, *L'Espace public*, ch. 7.

8. Ibid., p. 259.

9. Gabriel Tarde, *L'Opinion et la foule* (1901) (Paris: PUF, 1989).

Bibliography

. . . . .

Alberti, Leon Battista. *On Painting De Pictura*. Translated by John R. Spencer. Yale University Press, 1988.

Arendt, Hannah. *Between Past and Future: Eight Exercises in Political Thought*. Viking-Penguin, 1989.

Aristotle. *Metaphysics*. Translated by John McMahon. Prometheus Books, 1991.

——. *Nicomachean Ethics*. Translated by David Ross. Oxford University Press, 1998.

——. *Physics*. Edited by W. Charlton. Oxford University Press, 1990.

——. *Poetics*. Translated by Malcolm Heath. Viking-Penguin, 1997.

Augé, Marc. *An Anthropology for Contemporaneous Worlds (Mestizo Spaces)*. Translated by Amy Jacobs. Stanford University Press, 1999.

Barthes, Roland. *Camera Lucida: Reflections on Photography*. Farrar, Straus & Giroux, 1985.

Bataille, Georges. *Inner Experience*. Translated by Leslie A. Boldt. State University of New York Press, 1990.

Baudelaire, Charles-Pierre. *The Painter of Modern Life and Other Essays*. Edited by Jonathan Mayne. Phaidon, 1995.

Benjamin, Walter. *The Arcades Project*. Translated by Kevin McLaughlin and Howard Eiland. Harvard University Press, 1999.

——. *Illuminations*. Schocken Books, 1979.

——. *One-Way Street and Other Writings*. Verso, 1997.

Bourdieu, Pierre. *Photography: A Middle-Brow Art*. Translated by Shaun Whiteside. Stanford University Press, 1996.

Debord, Guy. *The Society of the Spectacle*. Translated by Donald Nicholson-Smith. Zone Books, 1995.

Farge, Arlette, *Subversive Words: Public Opinion in Eighteenth-Century France*. Translated by Rosemary Morris. Pennsylvania State University Press, 1995.

Foucault, Michel. *The Order of Things*. Vintage Books, 1994.

Francastel, Pierre. *Art and Technology in the Nineteenth and Twentieth Centuries*. Translated by Randall Cherry. Zone Books, 2000.

Freud, Sigmund. *Complete Works*. Edited by James Strachey. Norton, 1999.

Gidion, Siegfried. *Space, Time and Architecture*. Harvard University Press, 1988.

von Goethe, Johann Wolfgang. *Faust*. Translated by Randall Jarrell. Farrar, Straus & Giroux, 2000.

Gombrich, Ernst H. *Art and Illusion*. Princeton University Press, 2000.

Habermas, Jürgen. *Structural Transformation of the Public Sphere: An Inquiry into a Category of Bourgeois Society*. Translated by Thomas Burger. MIT Press, 1991.

Hegel, Georg Wilhelm Friedrich. *Phenomenology of Spirit*. Translated by J. N. Findlay. Oxford University Press, 1979.

——. *Philosophy of Right*. Translated by S. W. Dyde. Prometheus Books, 1996.

——. *Reason in History : A General Introduction to the Philosophy of History*. Prentice-Hall, 1953.

Heidegger, Martin. *The Fundamental Concepts of Metaphysics: World, Finitude, Solitude*. Translated by William McNeill. Indiana University Press, 2001.

Hesiod. *Theogony, Works and Days, Shield*. Translated by Apoltolos N. Athanassakis. Johns Hopkins University Press, 1990.

Hobbes, Thomas. *Leviathan*. Edited by C. B. Macpherson. Viking-Penguin, 1997.

Hugo, Victor. *Notre-Dame de Paris*. Translated by Alban Krailsheimer. Oxford University Press, 2000.

Kant, Immanuel. *Critique of Judgment*. Translated by J. H. Bernard. Prometheus Books, 2000.

———. *Critique of Pure Reason*. Edited by Paul Guyer and Allen W. Wood. Cambridge University Press, 1999.

———. *Foundations of the Metaphysics of Morals* and *What Is Enlightenment?* Translated by Lewis White Beck. Prentice-Hall, 1989.

Kierkegaard, Sören. *Fear and Trembling*. 15th ed. Translated by Alastair Hannay. Viking-Penguin, 1986.

Lanzmann, Claude. *Shoah: The Complete Text of the Acclaimed Holocaust Film*. 1st ed. Da Capo, 1995.

Laplanche, Jean, and Jean-Bertrand Pontalis. *The Language of Psycho-Analysis*. Translated by Donald Nicholson-Smith. Norton, 1974.

Leroi-Gourhan, André. *Gesture and Speech*. Translated by Anna B. Berger. MIT Press, 1993.

Lessing, Gotthold E. Ephraim. *Laocoon: An Essay on the Limits of Painting and Poetry*. Translated by Edward A. McCormick. Johns Hopkins University Press, 1990.

Marin, Louis. *On Representation*. Translated by Catherine Porter. Stanford University Press, 2001.

Merleau-Ponty, Maurice. *Phenomenology of Perception*. Translated by Colin J. Smith. Routledge, 1990.

Montaigne, Michel. *Complete Essays of Montaigne*. Stanford University Press, 1958.

Nancy, Jean-Luc. *Hegel: The Restlessness of the Negative*. University of Minnesota Press, 2002.

Nietzsche, Friedrich Wilhelm. *The Anti-Christ*. Translated by H. L. Mencken. Armonk, N.Y.: M. E. Sharpe, 1999.

Panofsky, Erwin. *Idea: A Concept in Art Theory*. Translated by Joseph J. Peake. HarperTrade Books, 1974.

Peirce, Charles S. *The Essential Writings*. Edited by Edward C. Moore. Prometheus Books, 1998.

Plato. *Plato's Parmenides*. Translated by R. E. Allen. Yale University Press, 1998.

Pliny, the Elder. *Natural History, a Selection*. Edited by John F. Healy. Vintage Books, 1991.

Proust, Marcel. *Remembrance of Things Past*. 3 vols. Translated by Terence Kilmartin and C. K. Scott-Moncrieff. Vintage Books, 1982.

Ricoeur, Paul. *Time and Narrative*. Vol. 1. Translated by Kathleen Blamey, David Pellauer, and Kathleen McLaughlin. University of Chicago Press, 1990.

de Quincy, A. C. Quatremere. *Essay on the Nature, the End, and the Means of Imitation in the Fine Arts*. Edited by Sydney J. Freedberg. Garland Press, 1979.

Saint Augustine of Hippo. *Confessions*. Translated by Henry Chadwick. Oxford University Press, 1998.

Valéry, Paul. *The Collected Works of Paul Valéry*. Vol. 1. Princeton University Press, 1971.

Vernant, Jean-Pierre. *The Universe, the Gods, and Men: Ancient Greek Myths*. Translated by Linda Asher. HarperCollins, 2001.

Vitruvius. *The Ten Books on Architecture*. Translated by Morris H. Morgan. Dover Books, 1950.

Warburg, Aby M. *Images from the Region of the Pueblo Indians of North America*. Translated by Michael P. Steinberg. Cornell University Press, 1997.

Index

· · · · ·

EUROPEAN PERSPECTIVES
A Series in Social Thought and Cultural Criticism
Lawrence D. Kritzman, Editor

. . . . .

Elisabeth Badinter   *XY: On Masculine Identity*

Karl Löwith   *Martin Heidegger and European Nihilism*

Gilles Deleuze   *Negotiations, 1972—1990*

Pierre Vidal-Naquet   *The Jews: History, Memory, and the Present*

Norbert Elias   *The Germans*

Louis Althusser   *Writings on Psychoanalysis: Freud and Lacan*

Elisabeth Roudinesco   *Jacques Lacan: His Life and Work*

Ross Guberman   *Julia Kristeva Interviews*

Kelly Oliver   *The Portable Kristeva*

Pierra Nora   *Realms of Memory: The Construction of the French Past*

> vol. 1: *Conflicts and Divisions*
>
> vol. 2: *Traditions*
>
> vol. 3: *Symbols*

Claudine Fabre-Vassas *The Singular Beast: Jews, Christians, and the Pig*

Paul Ricoeur   *Critique and Conviction: Conversations with François Azouvi and Marc de Launay*

Theodor W. Adorno   *Critical Models: Interventions and Catchwords*

Alain Corbin   *Village Bells: Sound and Meaning in the Nineteenth-Century French Countryside*

Zygmunt Bauman   *Globalization: The Human Consequences*

Emmanuel Levinas   *Entre Nous*

Jean-Louis Flandrin   *Food: A Culinary History* and Massimo Montanari

Alain Finkielkraut   *In the Name of Humanity: Reflections on the Twentieth Century*

Julia Kristeva   *The Sense and Non-Sense of Revolt: The Powers and Limits of Psychoanalysis*

Régis Debray   *Transmitting Culture*

Sylviane Agacinski   *The Politics of the Sexes*

Alain Corbin   *The Life of an Unknown: The Rediscovered World of a Clog Maker in Nineteenth-Century France*

Michel Pastoureau   *The Devil's Cloth: A History of Stripes and Striped Fabric*

Julia Kristeva   *Hannah Arendt*

Carlo Ginzburg   *Wooden Eyes: Nine Reflections on Distance*

Elisabeth Roudinesco *Why Psychoanalysis?*

Alain Cabantous *Blasphemy: Impious Speech in the West from the Seventeenth to the Nineteenth Century*

Julia Kristeva *Melanie Klein*

Julia Kristeva *Intimate Revolt and The Future of Revolt: The Powers and Limits of Psychoanalysis*, vol. 2

Claudia Benthien *Skin*